The Resource Handbook for Academic Deans

GEORGE ALLAN, EDITOR

ACAD

AMERICAN CONFERENCE
OF ACADEMIC DEANS

Editor: George Allan

A project of the
Board of Directors of the American Conference of Academic Deans

Production Editors:
Eliza Jane Reilly, Executive Director, ACAD
Rachel Riedner. Program Manager, ACAD

Copy Editor: Susan Reiss
Designer: Dee Bogetti

The American Conference of Academic Deans would like to thank Suzanne Hyers and Maria Helena Price, former Executive Officers of ACAD, under whose leadership this project was initiated and developed.

Published by
American Conference of Academic Deans
1818 R Street, NW
Washington, DC 20009

TABLE OF CONTENTS

iii

PREFACE

This Handbook, it says, is for Deans. The term "dean" is old wine that comes these days in many new bottles. You are to take it as a portmanteau word, a word, as Humpty Dumpty explained to Alice, capable of carrying a great number of diverse meanings. In this case, it does the work of a great diversity of titles for the senior academic officer of an institution of higher education: Vice Chancellor for Academic Affairs, Vice President for Academic Affairs, Provost, Dean of the College, Dean of the Faculty. Moreover, this Handbook may well be of help to those who are academic officers but not the senior academic officer. This would include associate or assistant deans who report to deans, deans who report to provosts, provosts who report to vice-presidents, and many another idiosyncratic expression of the organizational structure of an academic administration. Deans in all these senses serve at institutions with a great variety of ways by which to identify their genus: Academy, Community College, Junior College, Four-Year College, Technical College, Comprehensive College, College of a University, University, University System. The usual way in this Handbook has been to refer to

the institution of higher education as your "institution," but often as a "college" and sometimes as a "university." But whatever the name, whatever the locale: this Handbook is for those who toil in the vineyards of academe as the administrators responsible for overall management of the processes by which a faculty is recruited and developed and a curriculum fashioned and reformed as an instrument for the education of students and the furtherance of knowledge.

In 1992 members of the Board of Directors of the American Conference of Academic Deans (ACAD) decided it would be useful if there were a handbook that could help new deans adjust to the challenges and terrors of their new position. The men and women who find themselves holding appointments to major positions in academic administration are rarely aware of what their responsibilities involve. They may have thought they knew. But what from the outside, from the vantage point of a faculty member or a junior administrative position, may have seemed intelligible often turns out to be quite different when experienced from the inside. The responsibilities sketched in a job description and the procedures detailed in task booklets and tickler files are complicated, and the sheer volume of them can seem overwhelming. Far more daunting, however, is the interpersonal character of most of these responsibilities, calling for sensitivity, discretion, political acumen, moral insight, and prudential judgment.

The ACAD Board thought it would be helpful to put down on paper some of the words of advice experienced deans think their less experienced new colleagues would appreciate. This Resource Handbook is the result. The Board agreed that the handbook should be practical. There are plenty of other venues for providing interpretive frameworks, historical perspectives, psychological analyses, and hortatory expectorations regarding deanliness. And there are hundreds of monographs filled with the detailed technicalities of particular policies, programs, procedures, and pedagogical products. The Resource Handbook aims at the middle range: more general than the nitty-gritty, more specific than the theoretical. It is hoped that it will be something that new deans consult first when confronted with an issue they find perplexing. The Handbook is thus a bit like Dr. Spock, providing reassurances, indicating some preliminaries to be considered, suggesting where to acquire additional information.

The original idea had been that the Handbook might be written by one person, or maybe a troika of authors. But it was clear that no extant dean had either the wisdom or the time to pull this off. In June 1994, a committee composed of David Jordan (Austin College), Bari Watkins (Morningside College), and

myself as chair, undertook to draft a set of topics that the Board would then assign to various deans around the country based on their interest or expertise in a given area. Deans are busy people, however, and finding ones who would agree to take on a writing assignment, much less securing their drafts in timely fashion, proved to be very much like the proverbial difficulties involved in changing a curriculum. Eventually, however, the graveyard was moved and the cats herded across the road, and the results are now before you. Along the way, the pool of authors shrunk to be only slightly wider than the members of the Board.

An idea only accomplished in a few instances was to post drafts of the various discussions to the internet news group for academic deans which is run by ACAD. It was hoped that the wide variety of perspectives afforded by these colleagues would reap a bountiful harvest of further comments and critiques; some of these contributions could then be added to the author's original discussion. Unfortunately harried deans don't spontaneously put responses to e-mail requests for commentary at the top of their daily agendas, especially if the questions are complex and ask for more than the comparatively easy "at my institution we..." kind of response. Nonetheless, the Handbook has managed to include a few of these exchanges. They symbolize the way in which a Dean's Handbook should be a work in progress, a text always in need of glosses, commentaries, and addenda. You are encouraged to share your reactions with members of the ACAD Board or with the Washington D.C. office. It is hoped that such exchanges about the Handbook will soon require a Revised Edition, and in that edition that you will have become one of the voices in its ongoing conversation about the basic practicalities of academic administration.

Two lists are provided at the conclusion of this book. The first list contains the names of the Chairs of the ACAD Board over the years from the inception of the Handbook idea to its publication. They have had the interesting responsibility of being a cat herders' herder, patiently but persistently moving this project forward. The other list is of the authors of the 42 topics that comprise this Handbook. If academic deans are in any sense a community it is by virtue of their common loyalty to ideals of educational leadership and service. One exquisite evidence of this loyalty is their willingness to find the time to prepare their contributions to this Handbook, for they have done so without financial remuneration and without much expectation of anyone caring—except new deans, unknown to them, who will someday read what they have said, and maybe be helped by it. The deans appearing in these two lists are identified by the institution with which they were associated at the time of their contribution to this project.

George Allan
Handbook Editor
April 1998

1

What A Dean Is

ACAD

AMERICAN CONFERENCE
OF ACADEMIC DEANS

THE ETHICS OF DEANING

Charles D. Masiello, Pace University

INTRODUCTION

Albert Einstein believed that his era was characterized by the perfection of means and the confusion of ends. Times may not have changed much, but academic leaders bear a particular responsibility both to be clear about the ends they are striving to achieve and to be certain that the means to those ends are beyond reproach.

While some cynics may view an "ethical dean" as an oxymoron, your role as dean is critical in nurturing ethical behavior in your college or university. You stand at the nexus of the sometimes competing interests of administration, faculty, and students. You are called upon on a daily basis to make numerous decisions and must exercise Solomon-like wisdom to resolve complex issues that are apt to have significant consequences for the three groups cited, as well as for the future of the institution. Many, perhaps most, of these issues have an ethical

dimension that must square with the prevailing culture and your personal standards.

You are expected to present a balanced, equitable, and ethical perspective on all issues and to act accordingly. Unfortunately, such behavior on your part is often viewed by various constituencies as indicating your agreement with the positions they have advanced. This, of course, poses a dilemma for any ethical person holding the office of dean. How can you satisfy your own conscience, do the "right thing," and thereby feel good about your actions, while at the same time making those actions acceptable to the various constituencies served by your office, at least to the extent that your institution's survival and progress are insured?

Those of us who hold the title of dean know this dilemma all too well. Likely, there is no perfect answer to this question, but the following reflections may be helpful.

SOME THOUGHTS

Be clear in your own mind about your personal code of ethics. Remember the old admonition: know thyself! Be sure others know you too and what you stand for. Manifest your code of ethics in your behavior. Where appropriate and genuine, pick issues to air publicly that can illustrate your code of ethics.

Know the culture—or more likely cultures—within which you are functioning. Determine the extent to which your personal values coincide with prevailing convictions, especially those of the faculty and the president. If these two are irreconcilable, begin now to seek another position. You are in the wrong job or place. More likely, however, you will discover considerable but not complete overlap.

Examine present issues in light of both of the above admonitions. Measure them against your own standards and attempt to view them from the perspectives of other relevant and affected people or groups. Such reflection usually leads to insights that can be helpful in resolving even complex issues.

Remember Norman Vincent Peale's stress on the power of positive thinking. Do not become entangled in negative thinking, criticism, or action. Do not contribute to an atmosphere of suspicion or anxiety. Do not dwell on failings, but instead concentrate on strengths and use them to achieve a more effective organization.

Pope John XXIII, in another context, is reported to have expressed the view that one should see everything, overlook a great deal, and change a little. That is good advice for deans in most situations.

However, there may be times when you will want or need to change much. Be sure to do it judiciously, with skill, consultation, and adequate explanation. You will not be successful if you are unable to bring the community to share your perspective.

One of your principal tasks is to bring about the involvement of all relevant persons and groups in an issue, including its ethical aspects, and to develop as much agreement as possible. Having done that, it is your duty to make decisions in a timely fashion. Faculty members are trained to keep the question open, but administrators, by virtue of their responsibilities, need to decide and act within restricted time frames and often with incomplete data, making clear the fallibility but nonetheless the importance of such decisions.

Have faith in yourself and in your own judgment. Not everything can be decided on purely objective grounds; there are times when subjective judgment is necessary, even desirable. It falls to you as an academic leader to be scrupulously fair, consistent, and caring. You must also be responsive to various people and groups. But remember that responsiveness can mean saying no as well as yes.

Expect the best from yourself and others. It is your obligation to help others to realize their full potential. You also have a responsibility to yourself to provide enough time for reflection and physical activity to maintain your energy and creativity, not to mention your well-being.

People typically say they want a leader who will serve the common good, but they also want their parochial interests served.

It is your job to direct those special interests for the benefit of all. Of course the "common good" will be defined in different ways by different constituencies. But take heart, you as dean probably know more members of the academic community than any other person on campus. and you will be acutely aware of competing perspectives. You likely have broader experience in dealing with these constituencies as well. This gives you major advantages in defining the common good in a way that is acceptable to a broad spectrum of the community. Although special interest groups will evaluate you in terms of how often you agree with their perspectives, your ethical stance must be firm, consistent, and evident.

GUIDELINES FOR ETHICAL LEADERSHIP

❖ Listen before you act.
❖ Acknowledge the interdependence of the components of your institution.
❖ Consult with relevant individuals and groups.
❖ Take the time to be sensitive to your constituencies.
❖ Make every effort to serve their basic needs.
❖ Do not distort reality to achieve your own ends, even good ones.
❖ Correct misconceptions and incorrect interpretations.
❖ Respect others; do not diminish them in an attempt to make your point or win support for your perspective.
❖ Resolve rather than exploit conflict.
❖ Trust others until such time that they prove unworthy of your trust.
❖ Help others to realize their full potential.

❖ Set measurable and achievable goals.
❖ Provide the resources necessary for others to function effectively.
❖ Stand by others who in striving to meet common goals may make honest mistakes.
❖ Accept responsibility.
❖ Share the leadership task by empowering others.
❖ Take the blame; share the fame.

SOME FINAL ADVICE

Rules provide structure and guidelines, but in most instances they should not be followed slavishly. Prudent exceptions are provided for in good rules and are needed at times. For instance, in an effort to be fair, you may be tempted to treat every faculty member or student in the same way. But people are different and so are their individual circumstances. Even if they were not, you may have the opportunity to help only one or a few individuals of a given sort. Should you fail to extend that help for fear of not being able to assist all who are in similar circumstances? How often has it been said: "If I do it for you, I will have to do it for everyone?" Such a response, at least at times, can be totally inappropriate.

Insight into this apparent dilemma can be gained by taking an example from a completely different context: There are millions of starving children in this world. Would any of us fail to feed one of them if he or she came to us personally for help, for fear that we were being unfair to the others whom we could not feed? Yet in an academic setting we often feel that rules are sacrosanct. How many times do we resist helping one individual because of a distorted view of what fairness to the group or adherence to a rule means?

An ethical leadership response to a specific situation demands consideration of the human component and consequent action. You may not be able to do it for everyone, but you may be able to help the person who comes to you in need of assistance. If you can't, be honest about it without making excuses. That's part of ethical deaning!

To which Susan Gotsch (Hartwick College) adds:

But even while focusing on the needs of individuals in this way, be sure not to ignore issues of fairness and equity. The starving children may compare notes, so be prepared to justify your decisions or you may be accused (and maybe rightly) of favoritism.

And Gerald Lee Ratliff (Montana State University) remarks:

One of the first ethical concerns you will have is to decide how much information to share with department heads or faculty and in what context. Head's meetings and faculty meetings are traditionally the most visible forum to share ideas, outline new initiatives, clarify points of view and promote general consensus. There is also an inherent risk, however, that in those informal academic arenas you might be victimized by colleagues who apparently delight in seizing upon the public opportunity to question the content of your presentation, to challenge your point-of-view, or to debate the merits of a proposition under review without detailed information to reinforce or to support their individual argument(s). Ethics in this arena demands

that you disclose your primary sources, show potential relationships to current programs, and indicate long-range projections that may affect areas of immediate faculty concern. Ethics in the public forum demands that you be as open, honest, and inclusive as the issues allow. You ought also to be an attentive listener who respects differences of opinion. Your communicative posture should enrich faculty comprehension and understanding by including well-chosen examples, specific instances, and prescient symbols that help to amplify and to define the issue(s) being explored.

One of your ethical concerns should have to do with how best to resolve conflict. Conflict resolution demands that you have a broad-based, impartial perspective that separates fact from fancy in an active pursuit of the enduring truth which reconciles apparent differences of opinion on a selected issue. A primary guiding principle of conflict resolution is a willingness to entertain differing points of view and to arrive at an evenhanded, conciliatory judgment that best addresses the mutual interests of the parties concerned. Fair and open-minded deliberation and decision-making are especially important ingredients in any Dean's administrative strategy. Such qualities are the result of hard work: careful research of the problem area, detailed analysis of the potential implications of the problem area, and forward-thinking final recommendations that anticipate precise goals and objectives. When honesty and integrity inform your perspective on conflict resolution and also inform objective decision-making, your potential to be an effective and influential administrative leader is greatly enhanced.

COLLEGIAL RELATIONS

Len Clark, Earlham College

"What A Dean Is" can be answered by your college's organization chart, but of course the heart of a dean's professional identity consists in the relationships the dean inherits, and establishes, and nurtures.

RELATIONSHIPS WITH FACULTY COLLEAGUES

Veteran deans will tell you that the most radical and yet most subtle change you will experience in your relationships with others involves faculty colleagues. If you are a dean new to an institution, this is somewhat less dramatic because your acquaintance with new faculty colleagues will already be conditioned by their awareness of your role as dean. However, if you become a dean at the institution where you have been a faculty member, a cruel change occurs, the more difficult because it is so quiet. You will be tempted to think that the close friendships with 5 or 10 or

15 colleagues that have enriched your professional identity over the years can continue without radical change. Indeed, those colleagues will encourage you to believe that.

The change occurs because you will be less conscious of your "power" than are others. The sense (not at all necessarily matched in practice) that you are confiding in some members rather than others will set the faculty up for relationships of jealousy and lack of confidence in the ability of some to get a fair hearing from the dean. Continuing in the poker group you belonged to for years or the informal lunch group you've attended for a long time may not be impossible, but you will need to calculate the cost. Prepare to be brought up short sooner or later when a previously trusting colleague says to you, "You're not my colleague. You're the dean!"

The best protection against the difficulties of changed faculty/colleague relations is to go into the deanship knowing (at least intellectually) that they will happen and having determined this is a price you are willing to pay. It also helps to remember that there is not a sharp line between formerly allegedly apolitical relationships and new relationships defined by the politics of your role. We are colleagues still, and we never were friends who were unaware of each other's roles.

The final counsel on faculty relationships is that you should try hard to cultivate friendships with others outside the college community. The active cultivation of such friendships is an important dean's survival skill.

RELATIONSHIPS WITH OTHER ADMINISTRATORS

President. Of course, officially, your most important relationship is with the president or provost to whom you report. For most of us, this relationship begins in a healthy way because that person has chosen you as a colleague, presumably for good reasons! One of the clearest ways to maintain the confidence of this relationship is to be extremely careful about conversations outside the president's knowledge with members of the Board of Trustees. It's a good policy simply never to have conversations about business with Board members without reporting their substance to the president.

A second way to help nurture the relationship with the president is to make it a point to ask for a "reality check" about how you are doing every three months or so. Presidents are no better than the rest of us at providing systematic and frequent job performance feedback, especially on

points that may be awkward. Your willingness to open the context for such a discussion is thus all the more important.

Be especially careful to avoid discussions with faculty colleagues about the president. It will be especially tempting, and is especially dangerous, to confide that you share the faculty's position on an issue and will be trying to persuade the president, when you know the president may not be able to accept the position. Argue vigorously with the president in private, but remember that those same points made in public can easily appear to be undermining him or her.

Financial Vice President. This collegial relationship may be the most important of all, because the two of you will jointly be responsible for recommendations concerning faculty and staff compensation levels, tuition levels, and the amount of risk taking constituted by a particular year's budget. If the two of you do not have a high degree of confidence in one another, you face continual difficulties in interpreting the administration's stance, and the temptations of partisanship on behalf of each person's constituency will be difficult to resist. If the dean and the chief financial officer respect one another and can reach mutually acceptable positions without public confrontation, the two of you can protect the institution in times of presidential change or incapacity.

The most important condition for mutual trust between the CFO and the dean is ato develop a style of understanding one another that causes you not to need to take opposed positions in public. In most cases, when such oppositions get articulated, you will look the hero, and the CFO the villain. No one can tolerate being put in that position very often.

Other deans and vice presidents. These relationships are also crucial to the health of the institution. The chief peril in these relations is the assumption, made by faculty, that yours is the more important position. Yet the college requires that several departments and areas function effectively together in order for institutional goals to be met. The most successful deans are seen as supportive by their dean and vice presidential peers and are slow to assert seniority or authority. Close collegial relations—perhaps even professional friendships—among such administrative peers can become important sources of support, solace, and encouragement.

The relationships cultivated by the dean are crucial to the dean's success and that of the institution. The best counsel in all of them is to remember that everyone thinks you have more power than you do, and that perceived power generates fright and defensiveness. This will be true in the best deanships and the best managed institutions: it is an institutional reality. Build relationships of confidence by speaking softly, asserting authority with great infrequency, thanking your colleagues frequently, and praising their good work whenever the occasion arises.

Access to the Dean

George Allan, Dickinson College

How should a dean approach the question of "access"? Obviously someone can always make an appointment to see you, but are there ground rules your secretary should be instructed to use in making those appointments? Then there is the "just a quick question" ploy, the foot in the door that turns into an hour meeting. And there's telephone tag. And there's the problem of being inundated with hundreds of e-mail messages. How should you cope, shape, and control the processes by which others seek to gain access to you?

THE HALF-OPEN DOOR

You need to be—and you need to be perceived as being—available to faculty (and students and administrators and...). You also need to respond in timely fashion to whatever is asked of you by those who seek you out. This is a problem because the time taken up figuring out, through interactions with others, what you need

to do leaves too little time to get it done. This is especially true because what needs doing flows your way from formal initiatives (committees, departments, presidents) as well as from your more informal interactions with individuals. Indeed, there is an obvious inverse correlation (catch-22) here: the more you are open to others the more they ask of you, and hence the less time you have to do what they have asked you to do. Besides, you need time to plan your own initiatives, time to let your ideas ferment and to test them out through supposedly unproductive (informal) interactions, time to implement them in ways that are sometimes quite indirect and call for subtle constant fine tuning.

This is a demand and supply problem: the demand for your time is in excess of the supply you have of it. The solution, abstractly put, is obvious. On the demand side, reduce it by finding ways to avoid unnecessary meetings with others and by controlling the length of time each interaction requires. You need a sorting device to help you distinguish worthwhile from non-useful interactions and then to time those interactions accordingly: from "as long as it takes" to "go peddle your papers somewhere else." On the supply side, increase your availability by managing your time more cleverly and by delegating the responses to others. Think of associate deans, department heads, and committee chairs not just as lovable colleagues but also as extensions of yourself: Kant said it was okay to treat others as means as long as you also treat them as ends in themselves (use 'em but love 'em).

The preceding is easy to say in the abstract, difficult to translate into the routine practices of everyday deanship. But that's what they pay you the big bucks to do, right?

One reminder, however. One aspect of an educational institution is more important than its goals and the programs that implement those goals. This is its ethos, its style: the aesthetic and moral and interpretive framework within which your goals are formulated and pursued. One of your tasks as a dean is to nurture this ethos. Be sure that the way you find time for listening to others, making plans, and carrying them out also expresses this ethos. In a word, be sure that "how" you make yourself available to others exemplifies what it is to try and live by the ideals which originated and ground your institution's educational mandate.

SOME SPECIFIC COMMENTS AND SUGGESTIONS

Gil Atnip (Indiana University Southeast)

I have tried to maintain an open door practice, because I think it is important for faculty and staff to see me as accessible rather than as a remote "administrative other." Under that approach, the best way to handle the "quick question" is to let the person know you have limited time because of a meeting or whatever (assuming that is true) but that if the question can be handled quickly you will be happy to talk now. You can also put an end to a quick question session that turns into an hour with the same approach. On the other hand, I often learn some interesting things in those sessions that make them worthwhile (usually those have nothing to do with the original pretext of the conversation). The bottom line is that to maintain the openness that I want, I have had to give up some control over my time; I think it has been worth it. In fact, I often think I don't see enough faculty members in my office.

My predecessor in this job told me that the main qualification was to have the attention span of a three-year-old. I have found that he was right.

Harry L. Hamilton (Chapman University)

Inform your secretary of the length of time you will devote to the meeting and have her interrupt you at that point with "an emergency."

Have two addresses, one "unlisted" for key administrators to use in reaching you, the other for "the world" to use. Read the former, scan the latter for pithy info—such as ACAD messages!!!!

For people who try to end-run the system repeatedly, insist that their business can get to you only through their superior, who acknowledges that he/she has been unable to solve the problem. Other than that, just be obnoxious so no one *wants* to interact with you!!! (But you still have to get your job done!!)

Peter Alexander (Saint Peter's College)

People vary in their ability to resume work after an interruption and in their ability to chase someone out of the office when time is pressing. One's policy should take these things into account. I have no difficulty with interruption of written work and can resume immediately without problem. On the other hand, I can't cope with interruptions of budgetary work and tend to make errors when that sort of work is interrupted.

I have authorized my secretary to tell people that I will not see them or speak with them unless they state a purpose for their call or visit. If the caller insists that the matter is confidential, she will tell them that they must state the general nature or category of the problem without revealing any confidential details. All too often it turns out that the problem can be dealt with by the secretary.

Lisa A. Rossbacher (Southern Polytechnic State University)

Go meet faculty members in their offices, rather than having them come to yours. Although this isn't always possible or convenient, it offers a number of advantages.

The scenery is varied. *You* control the length of the meeting (it is far easier to excuse yourself and leave than to figure out a way to get someone else out your door). You see where and how faculty are working, and you learn more about them by seeing their books and materials. You see the physical condition of academic facilities. You are less likely to be interrupted by administrative colleagues. You break down the barriers that exist for some people in The Dean's Office (which can also be used to advantage, on occasion, as well). You see other faculty, staff, and students en route to and from the meeting (which requires allowing extra travel time!). And you are seen to be outside of your office.

James L. Pence (St. Olaf College)

I began five years ago with a system I learned from my dean: a combination of 1) established "staff conferences" with the people who report directly to me; 2) "open calendar" time initiated by others (for which I ask people to declare to my secretary the purpose of the meeting); 3) blocked out calendar time for uninterrupted work, wandering around, etc. 1) an 2) are going OK; 3) seems to erode (and I don't do enough to protect it). Mike Marty once told me that being dean means that you can't keep up with your writing, then you can't keep up with your reading, then you can't keep up with your thinking..... Protecting time for reading, writing, and thinking for me means blocked out calendar time.....

Karl Reitz (Wilkinson College of A & S, Chapman University)

If I were to give away the resources I have and empower others to accomplish what I can accomplish, then there would be less need for others to try to go through me to get resources or power.

John Churchill (Hendrix College)

My best hunch is that devices for controlling access are far less important than the dean's ability to use ten and fifteen minute segments of time well, his or her ability to hold multiple projects in view and to keep moving them along as opportunity presents itself to touch this one, then that one, next the other, and so on. A few years ago we had a visiting troupe of Chinese acrobats on campus. They did amazing things—stacking chairs, juggling knives, tumbling. But one act really seized me. A guy came out and set up a series of thin poles, atop each of which he set a plate spinning. He set up more and more poles, with more and more plates, and as the new ones went up, the old ones began to wobble and he'd give the pole a twist and set things right and then a new pole with a new spinning plate would go up but then three plates on old poles would start to wobble and they'd get tweaked and a new pole would go up and the audience would gasp as five old poles would start to go and—quick—in the nick of time he'd save them and put up some more, and so on and on. It looked like my job—only between poles he should have been interviewing candidates.

The moral is this: the job is intrinsically incoherent in its daily texture. The coherence has to come from somewhere besides the rhythm of the day's work.

Paul Formo (Dana College)

I agree with the several comments made with regard to walking around and have one small contribution (gimmick) to add at this point. I am not sure where I learned it, but it is not an original idea— the "stand up meeting." It is a very useful way of handling the "one quick question" and it works simply by not sitting down as they come in and not inviting them to sit down. One can be very friendly and cordial anyway, but it is amazing how discussing the issue while standing shortens the time on the topic.

Stephen Briggs (Rollins College)

My secretary uses a simple strategy to protect my time for special projects, planning, grant writing, and so on as well as for returning memos, e-mail, and phone calls. I get to work early and she schedules no appointments until 10 a.m. I use the time to deal with the mail and phone piles from the previous day and (ideally) longer term projects. She also assesses how far above or below water I am and schedules additional work periods (2 to 3 hours periodically) so that I can catch up or deal with an important matter.

Management Techniques

Martha Crunkleton, Bates College

In a recent flurry of postings to the ACAD discussion listserve, there were many comments about particular management techniques and their effectiveness in Academia as well as general comments about whether the very word management had any cash value in higher education. Some thought that the word itself would send colleagues into a tizzy because it was inherently evil!

Perhaps they are right. Whatever management technique one subscribes to, some of the issues around being a dean have more to do with self-management than with "managing" or "not appearing to manage" others.

What I have spent lots of time on as dean is the kind of thing that one finds in the *I Ching*—avoid mentally executing one's enemies; the mark of the great leader is that the people say "we did this ourselves;" and, not every thought must be articulated--and in Pascal--all of mankind's troubles come from our inability to sit in a small room by ourselves.

Listening 101 is the course I most often wish I could take. Perhaps a remedial course would be "Point of View: How to Spot Your Own and How To Learn to Respect Other's." From the moon, the Paris zoo and the Louvre appear to be side-by-side, I guess; in Paris, they are somewhat farther apart.

Apart from the appropriate control of the self (that is, dismissing mental chatter and learning to be skeptical about believing in the phantasms created by Ego), the study of time management and of conflict facilitation would be helpful to new deans. I have done the latter, and it has helped me enormously. The former I have also studied, so far to no apparent gain.

Here are some pragmatics about management that new deans may find helpful:

❖ Have chairs meet regularly and ask the chairs to submit agenda items that you then take up first in the meeting.

❖ Encourage departmental or program retreats; this is the one device I have used at Bates that I can tell has helped departments and programs the most.

❖ Ask the faculty to evaluate you, confidentially, without their names, once a year.

❖ Announce good news about faculty and students every month at the faculty meeting.

❖ Try to avoid holding any meeting without an agenda, with time limits being distributed in advance. Time is the most valuable resource the faculty has—it should not be abused with meetings that waste time.

❖ Within the bounds of copyright law, try to circulate to the faculty as many articles and essays as possible about what is going on elsewhere at comparable and noncomparable institutions.

❖ Try to circulate the most thoughtful criticisms of higher education (not all our critics are mean-spirited or wrong) to faculty members as well as proud letters from parents, alumni/alumnae, friends of the college.

❖ Try to leave blocks of time in your calendar to get the writing done and to deal with emergencies.

❖ Try to meet with people in their office, not yours.

❖ Go to as many athletic contests and artistic performances as possible so that those faculty members who are coaching, directing, and conducting know that you understand the demands on the time and appreciate what they are doing for your students.

❖ Return all telephone calls from trustees and from foundation program officers within 30 minutes.

❖ When faculty members are angry, take the time to listen and do not defend yourself.

❖ Understand that your secretary or administrative assistant is 10 times more important to the working of the faculty and the college than you will ever be.

❖ Despite being overwhelmed with the furious tedium of the urgent but unimportant (sometimes, when I am listening to colleagues go on and on about something that most people I know outside higher education would consider petty, I have to forcibly restrain myself from asking them what they think about Bosnia, Rwanda, or the gutting of the public schools in the United States), try to remember every day the intrinsic value that the furious tedium matters, and that being a little helper to the faculty as their dean matters.

I have taped in my desk drawer advice I got from a book about President Truman. I read these 17 words at least two dozen times a day to stop my own mental chatter. Here they are:

✔ Work Hard
✔ Do Your Best
✔ Speak the Truth
✔ Assume No Airs
✔ Trust in God
✔ Have No Fear

If I were to try to improve on what President Truman said, I would add, "Laugh," but that may be implicit in not assuming airs. Whatever advice you find helpful, I urge you to place it where you can read it frequently.

So Now You Are A Dean: The First 100 Days

Douglas Steeples, Mercer University

The following remarks will apply best to you if you assume your deanly responsibilities on or about July 1, when most administrative contracts take effect. The advantages of a summer start are many. Perhaps the greatest is that at most institutions summer is a relatively "slow" time, which will grant you considerable time to acquaint yourself with a new institutional environment and responsibilities before the beginning of the academic year. If you assume your position at the middle of, or at some other point during, the academic year, you will need to accomplish many of the things outlined below while fulfilling your regular academic-year duties. Even so, the outline of activities delineated here can be modified to fit almost any starting date. It can also be adapted to fit local variations in circumstances.

SETTING THE TONE OF YOUR ADMINISTRATION: BEGINNING THE GAME

The greatest challenge facing you at the outset of your deanship or vice presidency will be to gain as rapidly as possible a comprehensive view of your institution, your college or school, key colleagues, and chief policies and procedures. Of no less importance will be the steps you take to establish the "tone" of your office. Will you present yourself as one prepared for the position? As knowledgeable about the leading issues and challenges with which you will have to deal? As authoritarian or open? As a speaker only, or as one who can listen and reflect as well as speak and decide? As one who appreciates the importance of respecting lines of communication and authority while understanding also the importance of being available when appropriate? As an open-door or a closed-door administrator? As one who rarely leaves the office, or as one who "walks around"?

During the first 100 days you will, consciously or not, establish the precedents that will create enduring perceptions among your colleagues of what they can expect of you. You will also lay the foundations for the most important working relationships with which you will be bound. It is critically important, then, that you do everything possible to create the conditions for success. It may not hurt, either, to remember that as one wise old dean put it, academic administration is a bit like a poker game, but with one important difference: upon assuming your position as a new dean or chief academic officer, you buy into the local game and receive a stack of chips. But you almost never win chips. Instead, you spend them. If you are careful, effective, and fortunate, you can spend them very slowly. Nevertheless there will probably come a time when they are all spent, and it is time to find a new game.

There are some important things that you can do to buy the largest possible initial stack of chips, and become prepared to spend them wisely, and slowly:

GETTING A "TAKE" ON YOUR INSTITUTION: READING

Although you will have read through a great deal of material in the course of your candidacy and the selection process, there are few better ways to spend your time at the outset of a deanship or academic vice presidency than in reading carefully through selected materials. You may never again have the time to do so. It will be important to review in detail at least the following, in order to firm up your understanding of the modes of operation of the most pressing issues facing, and the matters lately dealt with by, your school or college. At the very least, then, you will want to read with care:

❖ The college bulletin/catalog, viewbook, and other admissions materials:
  ◆ complete a "course count" as a means of getting a curricular overview;
  ◆ complete a staffing diagram to give you a sense of how your human resources are allocated;
  ◆ frame an understanding of whom the institution seeks to recruit as students, and how.
❖ The minutes for at least the most recently completed academic year, of the faculty business meeting or that of the faculty senate or equivalent.
❖ The records or recommendations of any committees on faculty recruitment, promotion, and tenure, together with those of your predecessor.
❖ The records for the past year of any other committees that work closely with you.
❖ The faculty handbook, especially those portions pertaining to the practices in place for recruiting, promoting, and tenuring faculty colleagues, and those pertaining to faculty responsibilities, and to processes for changing the curriculum.
❖ The most recently completed accreditation self-study report, and written responses and recommendations from your regional accrediting body.
❖ The budgets for your college or school at least for the current and the most recent year, and, if possible, three to five years, in order to ascertain trends.
❖ Audited financial statements for your college or school.

❖ Any written materials concerning budget planning procedures and processes, and policies governing fiscal management.

❖ Any college, school, or (especially) presidential planning documents.

GETTING A "TAKE" . . . MEETING PEOPLE

You may be surprised to discover, if you are new at deaning, how quickly people find you once you have arrived. It is not uncommon to discover that every department chair within a school or college will possess, or contrive, some legitimate reason to call on you during your first weeks in the office. This is apt to be no less true in summer than at other points during the year. You will find it very helpful to frame a systematic approach to meeting people who will be important for your, and your school's or college's, success. Long years of experience recommend prioritizing opportunities to meet with people, in order to begin to build working relationships. There is much to be said for meeting with them on their own turf, in their own offices, at least initially. Doing so will send an important message about your accessibility. It will also grant you a direct view that can be gained in no other way.

❖ Confer first with your secretary and establish a clear understanding about how you wish the office to operate. Do you want to be interrupted by phone calls while conversing with people (generally, no!)?

❖ Which box is for "in" and which for "out" mail? Should the secretary prescreen your mail?

❖ Will your door be open or closed, and when?

❖ Can the secretary make use of the secretarial network to keep you informed of potential problems?

❖ Does your secretary know what areas have been problematic for the previous occupant of your office?

❖ From which sources or directions may one expect difficulties?

❖ Confer with the person to whom you report. Undoubtedly you will have conversed during the search process about your working relationship. It is important to follow up and clarify mutual expectations. Is a weekly written report of your actions desired? How often should you debrief? Will the person to whom you report desire regularly scheduled meetings, or does this person manage time in such fashion as to feel (and be) free to call you in at any time, no matter what you are doing or with whom you might be meeting? (This is a delicate issue, to be handled cautiously, but it is important.)

❖ Confer with your department chairs, one by one, and listen as they respond to an invitation from you to describe their needs, hopes, problems, and so on.

❖ If there is a council of chairs that meets regularly, meet with it and through open conversation establish shared expectations about what it will do, and how.

❖ If there is a standing committee of the faculty that exists to advise you, meet with it and listen with care as its members talk about how it works, what its concerns are. If there is not such a body, consider whether or not there ought to be, but keep your thoughts to yourself. Meet similarly with any other committees that will work closely with you and discuss openly their sense of constitutional and customary practice, and establish a basic understanding about your intended working relationship with them.

❖ Meet with the search committee, and again listen as you give it an opportunity to review its hopes, expectations, and so on. It has a stake in your success, as do your other constituencies, but its stake is larger and more direct. Consider how to use it, informally, but within the framework of existing college or school structures.

Depending on the size of your faculty, you may wish to announce and make arrangements to begin a series of office calls, one by one, on your entire faculty, to become acquainted and establish your availability, as well as to gain a sense of who your colleagues are. Some deans find it preferable to review personnel files before such visits; others, after. Wherever a program of visits is possible, it will very likely prove to be highly productive.

Don't forget Lawrence Peter "Yogi" Berra's axiom: "You can do a lot of observing just by watching." And Listen, Listen, Listen.

TEMPTATIONS TO RESIST DURING THOSE FIRST 100 DAYS

If you can avoid the following during the first 100 days you will have established some operating principles that will serve you well throughout your term:

1. Do not redecorate your office. Attend to business, and let decorating happen later.

2. Do not refer to your former institution by name, ever, if you can help it.

3. Do not fail to thank all who contribute to the work of your school or college.

4. Do not fail to acknowledge, publicly, the accomplishments of your faculty colleagues, regularly and often.

5. Do not allow paperwork to divert your attention from your job, which is (a) to provide the best possible education to your students, (b) by securing and "caring for" the best possible faculty

6. Do not allow yourself to be drawn into the practice of making hasty decisions where delay is possible, and do not make decisions affecting people without first conversing with them.

7. Do not change messages to fit audiences. Inconsistency is quickly equated with dishonesty or worse.

8. Do not use e-mail or memoranda where a phone call, or even better, a personal conversation, may be possible.

9. Do not take yourself, or your office, too seriously. When you err (and you will, if you are doing the job), own up to it at once, and retain an ability to laugh at yourself.

10. Do not forget that your have become a "larger" figure than you were in the past. What was vigorous debate when you were a professor becomes intimidation when you assume a dean's mantle. What was professorial license to express your feelings becomes a frightening and unseemly display of anger when you are a dean. Even for those who were your intimates before.

11. Like it or not, do not forget that you have become "one of them." No matter how broad and intimate your previous

array of faculty friendships, it can never be the same again.

12. Do not miss the opportunity to give reports at the regular meetings of your faculty, faculty senate, or equivalent. This practice affords you a wonderful opportunity to teach your faculty colleagues, but only if you embrace this task in a properly respectful spirit.

13. If you discover that there may be value in creating a periodic internal news publication from your office, do not assign it a pretentious name. The pathway to ditches containing the decaying remains of former deans and chief academic officers is cluttered with fragments of paper bearing names such as "Deanogram No. 213."

14. Do not forget the saying that a dean, or a chief academic officer, is to faculty as a fire hydrant is to a dog. Or deaning is often defined as an instance of the incompetent attempting to lead the ungovernable. Or as the equivalent of attempting to herd cats…. Remain, in short, realistic about the impossible.

Congratulations. You've now completed your first 100 days. May your experience now let you successfully complete many more.

COMMENTS

Lloyd W. Chapin (Eckerd College)

I like Doug Steeples's advice to new deans—both content and format. One suggestion regarding the reference to using up one's chips. There is a certain grim truth to this, but I think it should be balanced—as it is to some degree in the later "list"—by pointing out that there are

things one can do to replenish one's reservoir of good will by such things as abiding by policies, expressing gratitude often, operating with integrity, getting important things done that benefit the institution and the faculty as a whole.

One item to add to the advice list: When you hear a complaint about someone else to which you feel an obligation to respond, always tell yourself that there are at least two sides to every story and that you need to learn as nearly as possible the whole truth before rendering judgment or taking action.

David Hoekema (Calvin College)

I offer a few mildly dissenting comments on Doug Steeples's advice for new deans, most of which seems to me very much on target:

2. Do not refer to your former institution by name. Ever, if you can help it.

   I understand the point here. But this needs to be taken with a grain of salt: why did they hire you if not in order to bring to pass at this one some of the wonderful things you accomplished at your former institution? I think it's possible to make reference to other institutions' policies without suggesting that you are trying to force your new home into their mold.

8. Do not use e-mail or memoranda where a phone call, or even better, a personal conversation, may be possible.

   Huh? This goes against the principle of managing time to keep from getting bogged down. Moreover, a written memo has greater weight in memory than an e-mail note, which in turn has more than a conversation: make these differences work for you, not against you.

10. Do not forget that you have become a "larger" figure.... Even for those who were your intimates before.

11. Like it or not, do not forget that you have become "one of them."

I think these vary greatly with institutional climate. Again, what is needed are discretion and a keen sense for how things are taken. Taking this advice too seriously in some contexts will only create an air of aloofness. (And it sometimes seems to me that the way Calvin's administrative structure manages to avoid this gulf and to encourage close and congenial relationships between deans and faculty colleagues is (1) to make most decanal appointments by rotation from the faculty ranks (I was the first academic dean to be hired from outside) and (2) to give deans so little power that it isn't worth the trouble of brown-nosing . . .).

14. Do not forget the saying that a dean, or a chief academic officer, is to faculty as a fire hydrant is to a dog....

OK, OK, but I grow weary of these cynicisms. If the job isn't genuinely rewarding, if you don't sense that you are really helping junior faculty shape their careers and helping all faculty nurture intellectual and spiritual growth in students, if you don't feel an important and valued part of the institution—then do something else. The level of effort needed to be an effective dean isn't worth it if you are continually frustrated—and if you feel you are getting nowhere, month after month, you may well be right. Academic administration seems to be a career that often leads to interesting next jobs for those who decided it isn't quite right for them.

But if you want another proverb, one I prefer, and one whose source I cannot trace: "The job of the faculty is to think for the college; of the president, to speak for the college; of the dean, to keep the faculty from speaking and the president from thinking." All right, there's a touch of cynicism there too—my apologies. It's Monday, after all.

2

Becoming
A Dean

ACAD

AMERICAN CONFERENCE
OF ACADEMIC DEANS

Evaluating Deans

David Hoekema, Calvin College

Periodic and thorough review of performance, with provisions for feed back to the person evaluated and for appropriate action, is an area where academic institutions exhibit considerable inconsistency. For faculty members, the procedures for reappointment and tenure are nearly always spelled out in detail in the faculty handbook, and few department chairs or administrators take these rules lightly. (None take them lightly, one could almost conjecture, more than once.) For administrative staff, there is less consistency, but anecdotal evidence I have seen suggests that increased demands for accountability and efficiency have led to more frequent and more candid performance reviews on many campuses. For department chairs and heads of programs in the academic domain, procedures may be looser, but at a minimum there is almost invariably a formal process for renewal every three to five years that offers those who work under the individual's supervision to tell the college how well or how badly the work is being done.

But pity yourself, poor dean! Seldom overwhelmed with displays of affection and appreciation either from the faculty or from the president or vice president to whom you report, you toil on in tireless dedication but often in ignorance of how your work is assessed. Even when you serve for a specific and renewable term of office, the renewal process is often pro forma. Responses to the query posted on the ACAD list disclosed that relatively few academic deans feel they receive the level or the kind of periodic assessment that would enable them to carry out their responsibilities better—or, in extreme cases, to know when to pack their bags and leave town quietly. But you should take comfort in the realization that, even if academic administrators are seldom given regular performance review, the crime of decanicide appears to be rare.

In my own posting on this topic I wrote, "My sense is that colleges have tolerably good procedures for chair and program head evaluations, or at worst they know what they ought to do but do it half-heartedly. Evaluations of those with institution-wide responsibilities is at the same time much more important and much more difficult to do well." A review of other responses supports this impression. I excerpt several of them below.

What is it to conduct an evaluation of an academic dean in a thorough and helpful way? It is to have a process that balances various areas of responsibility, that rewards the righteous and punishes the wicked, and that also helps move the institution forward in pursuit of its goals. I cannot honestly say that I have seen such a process in operation in any institution where I have worked. During the eight years that I headed a national disciplinary association, I repeatedly asked the chair of the Board of Officers to conduct a comprehensive performance review, but it never happened, and I wondered why. The reasons, I concluded, must involve two factors: a belief that most of my work was being done so well that it was pointless to devote a lot of time to giving me a pat on the back; and an impression that the rest of my work was being botched so badly that it must surely represent deep-seated character defects that it is wisest not to dredge up and display for all to see. Perhaps the same two factors motivate the comparative neglect of evaluation for deans.

But before turning over the floor to colleagues, I want to say a word about one comprehensive performance review that I went through recently. Without wishing to wallow in self-pity, let me simply say that it left me profoundly discouraged in ways that I do not believe either those who submitted comments or the person who collated and summarized them had intended. In the end some good came of the process, but it happened in spite of, not because of, the way it was structured. A major problem, I believe, was the fact that comments were anonymous all round—no signatures that would help the person who collected them place them in context. A wiser course, I think, is to require signed comments and then let the person conducting the evaluation collate, summarize, and "anonymize."

Since we have not changed our process, I am undermining it by example as best I can. Every time I submit a performance evaluation, I send a copy to the subject, even if it contains pointed criticism. The response has been surprise, sometimes a bit of defensiveness, and then an eagerness to talk more about how to solve the problems. My administrative colleagues seem to agree that it would be a fine thing if this were to become a common practice. Which is not to say that any of them is dumb enough to follow my example, however.

Good evaluation procedures do a lot more than correct problems. They maintain a sense of collaboration and common purpose, and they help shape and form an institutional ethos of respect and accountability. They probably also reduce cholesterol and cure psoriasis.

Let me close with an observation from another realm. A close friend has undergone regular evaluations as an associate at two law firms. A partner was assigned to collect comments, most but not all, of which were cc'd to to my friend. The partner reviewed them for her a couple of weeks later, stated the criticisms candidly, but also conveyed an overall sense of strong support for her work which reassured her that she was in the right firm and on the right track in overall professional development. At another firm, everything was anonymous and she received no copies. For months after they were solicited, she heard nothing; finally the lawyer assigned to collate them returned her phone calls and arranged a meeting, at which she received positive but not very specific feedback. The first firm, one surmises, will have a much easier time recruiting and retaining excellent lawyers. As the Good Book says, go thou and do likewise, all ye who are presidents, vice presidents, or deans.

But to you who are new deans, at institutions where evaluation procedures of "first firm"quality are not in place, don't rush in where angels fear to tread (that's not from the Good Book but it sounds like it, right?). Give some careful thought to what you think is needed, as a reform of existing procedures or as something bright and spanking new. Then proceed to involve both your president and key faculty (e.g., your faculty personnel committee) in the refinement of your idea and eventually in its implementation. Remember that this evaluation procedure needs to be one designed not just for your needs but for those of your successors, yea even unto the seventh generation.

And now for some comments from colleagues on the ACAD list. I begin with three models for dean evaluation proce-

dures, then move to some improvisations on those models.

MODEL PROCEDURE NO. 1

Tom Wiltshire (Culver-Stockton College)

Quoting from my faculty handbook, a section called "Policies And Procedures For Evaluation of The Dean of The College":

> The evaluation shall take place at the end of March each year.
>
> A special survey instrument developed by the Committee on Faculty and the Dean of the College and approved by the President shall be employed in the evaluation process.
>
> The chairperson of the Committee on Faculty shall see to the distribution of the survey to all faculty members and the collection of the survey. Once the chair has collected the survey, it is to be shared with the President of the College, who will, in turn, share the survey with the Dean of the College.

In the evaluation of the Dean of the College, additional feedback should be sought from the professional staff, President's Cabinet, Division Chairpersons, and selected students.

MODEL PROCEDURE NO. 2

Peter Alexander (St. Peter's College)

A new process for evaluation of deans and other academic administrators was instituted in this past year:

1. The person to be evaluated submits a written, comprehensive self-evaluation to his/her superior.

2. Administrator meets with superior to review self-evaluation.
3. Superior writes a formal reaction to the self-evaluation.
4. Administrator writes a set of goals for the coming year.
5. The intent is that the next evaluation cycle will use fulfillment of these goals as the major premise of evaluation.

We haven't gotten to Step 5 as yet, so it is not possible to gauge the long-term efficiency of this process, although I'm pleased with what I've seen thus far.

MODEL PROCEDURE NO. 3

Susan Crockett (Syracuse University)

At Syracuse University, we have a system of periodically (approximately every five years) evaluating deans and senior administrators. This is run from the office of the Vice Chancellor of Academic Affairs (VCAA) for deans and the office of the Chancellor for senior administrators. The dean or administrator being evaluated submits a list of names (15-30) of people who are able to evaluate his or her work. The list can include faculty, Board of Visitors, other administrators at the university, students, and professionals outside the university. Then the VCAA or chancellor makes a list. The supervisor and person being evaluated agree on a list of evaluators. Then a letter is sent to each person asking for their evaluation and enclosing two documents, "Policy for the Formal Evaluation of Academic Administrators" and "Review of Senior Academic Administrators." Each evaluator is told to address the VCAA or Chancellor, label the evaluation "Personal and Confidential," and is told that only paraphrases, "carefully

structured to prevent identification of the source," will be shared with the individuals.

Evaluators are asked to indicate the interests, perspectives, or concerns that have shaped their relationship with the individual; to comment on accomplishments, opportunities, failures, or unsolved problems in institutional progress, administrative achievements, and intellectual and professional achievements; and to characterize the individual's working style, strengths and weaknesses in leadership, management skills, and communication skill.

The dean or senior administrator being evaluated is asked to supply a written self-review in light of the expectations for the office, the goals of the unit, and the activities of the recent years.

Last, the VCAA or chancellor meets with the individual to discuss the evaluations, self-assessment, and annual reports. Together they formulate goals for improvement if that is needed.

IMPROVISATION NO. 1

Martha Crunkleton (Bates College)

There is no procedure at Bates for evaluating deans. Since I arrived here in 1991, I send each year a copy of a simple evaluation form that I wrote to all members of the faculty and to all staff members who report to me for them to analyze my performance anonymously. I read these evaluations during the summer; after a period of contemplating resigning and/or suicide, I then take from these evaluations the truly constructive advice they frequently provide. I have learned many things from this process, some of which I will summarize here:

1. No one on the faculty knows what my job is;
2. Many faculty members use the evaluation as a way to let off steam and vent and to display their rhetorical flair and athleticism;
3. Many faculty members offer genuinely useful criticism and advice to me anonymously that they would not/could not tell me to my face or in a signed letter;
4. Many faculty members, including those who are most critical of me and think I should not be dean, have praised this process of requesting evaluations from them, especially in the faculty committee that meets with the Board of Trustees; and
5. Staff members seem to think I am doing a better job than faculty members do. My colleagues on the senior staff, as well as the president, do not think it is wise for me to do this but I persist. Depressing as it can be, it is helpful to me. It might be helpful to the people on the faculty and staff—I'm nor sure about that.

IMPROVISATION NO. 2

David Deal (Whitman College)

At Whitman we have no procedure in place. A couple of years ago I invited to campus a review team to review me and my office. They spent two days on campus and talked to everyone in sight and then wrote a report directly to the president. They also sent me a copy which I shared with the division chairs. The review team consisted of the deans at Carleton, Pomona, and Grinnell. I found their review

extremely helpful since they all knew what deaning means.

IMPROVISATION NO. 3, WITH CYNICAL CODA

Stephen Good (Drury College)

I am evaluated (my initiative) once every three or four years. The last time, I had the evaluations turned in to the president's office and collated them. Then I shared the results with our three elected division chairs (faculty) and asked them to help me interpret them. I did this partly for their insights and wisdom, partly for the message to the faculty that I was really listening and taking the evaluation seriously.

The evaluation was positive and affirming. After talking with the division chairs for some time about the evaluation, I asked what suggestions they had to improve my evaluation. One of them said, "Time the next evaluation right after the faculty gets a substantial raise." It was clear to them and to me that faculty concerns about the institution get reflected in the evaluation of the dean's performance (this would probably be true for the president or any other chief administrative officer).

VARIATIONS ON THE THEME OF CYNICISM

Peter Facione (Santa Clara University)

I have been deaning for 13 years and have been "evaluated' by a formal process three times. In each case, even when the results have been very gratifying and affirming, it has seemed to me that few, if any, in the process as opinion-givers, data-interpreters, recommenders, or

29

Becoming
A Dean

evaluators really know what deaning is about. Mostly this is not a criticism, for none of them has ever had to step up and dean.

The suggestion of getting an outside review team of other deans sounds like the best idea I've heard in a long time. Such a group could not only evaluate the dean, but evaluate the dean in the context of the particular institutional setting (with all that implies) and make recommendations not only to the vice president and president, but to the dean as well.

[Don't we know enough about human dynamics to realize that "evaluating the dean" conceived as an isolated evaluation of one person's performance is nearly impossible? At times it seems that the same person might be a wonderful success at one institution and a dreadful failure in another.]

EXERCISE FOR THE READER

How would you evaluate this handbook section on evaluating the dean? (Hint: begin by appointing a three-member ad hoc committee.)

Teaching and Research

Virginia Coombs, Oklahoma City University

Is it realistic for you to continue to teach or sustain an active research program after becoming dean? What things should you consider in deciding how best to answer this perplexing question?

In assessing the possibilities of continuing to teach and sustain an active research program, you must assess what your ultimate professional goals are: returning to the faculty after a period of administrative service or developing a career in academic administration. You must also take into consideration the context in which your administrative work occurs, i.e., whether you are the chief academic officer for the institution or whether you report to a provost or vice president.

Most colleagues support the concept that the role of the dean is most successfully carried out if one has come from the faculty ranks. As a member of a faculty, the dean is more in tune with the daily demands of teaching, advising, professional development, and campus service. Deans who lose touch with these faculty interests may not be as effective in promoting faculty welfare with the other members of the administration. The responses from the ACAD Deans Discussion list suggest that continued involvement in teaching and research is a matter of degree and highly dependent on institutional context.

If, as some colleagues maintain, you are "on loan" from the faculty for the period during which you serve as dean, the terms of that "loan agreement" should clearly state the expectations with regard to teaching and research activities. Some—but by no means all—of the questions which need to be settled up front are:

1. Is teaching considered an integral part of your position or as an overload, i.e., to be accomplished around the fringes of administrative work?
2. What are the expectations for continuing research? Are there funds for you to attend at least one professional

disciplinary conference each year? Is there the possibility of you having a sabbatical for research after the appropriate period of service?

3. How will your "faculty duties" be assessed and evaluated in the context of your administrative position?

4. If you have come from outside the institution without tenure, is tenure possible? What procedures will be used to determine tenure?

You must assess for yourself whether this set of conditions will permit full participation in the administration as well as participation as a faculty member. Indeed, on many campuses this is exactly the model used for the position of associate dean. Where the "on loan" model applies to the dean, the institution must be comfortable with the philosophy that academic administration can be accomplished by rotating individuals through the dean's office.

Many colleagues see the value in you maintaining some regular contact with the classroom. After all, it is here that you encounter the reason your institution exists—the students. Having regular classroom contact with the students in your college or university provides you with a much better sense of how its educational programs are working. You can maintain this contact if you regularly teach a course in your own discipline, participate in interdisciplinary courses, team teach with other faculty members, or make guest appearances in classes. These activities will help to keep your teaching skills active and demonstrate to both students and faculty members that the dean plays a role in the classroom scene. In addition to the usefulness of teaching, there is this intrinsic value: you entered higher education,

after all, committed to teaching and scholarly pursuits, and to interaction with students.

Maintaining an active research program appears to be not as easily achievable as regular participation in the classroom. Many deans suggest that, in addition to conducting research in the discipline in which one received graduate training, you should do research on topics in higher education administration. These are the topics—budget, enrollment management, program assessment, etc.—that consume your daily administrative work and so provide the basis for an expertise that should find scholarly expression.

There are no easy answers to this question of maintaining an active teaching and research program while carrying an administrative workload. Here are the responses from some of your colleagues:

Rich Millman (Whittier College)

If you plan to make a career in deaning, and possibly presidenting, then some research/teaching tapering off makes sense. If you really want to return to the faculty some day (or it is too early to make a decision), then stay with some teaching (one course a year is max) and stay current.

David H. Goldenberg (The Sage Colleges)

I hope the day never comes when I think of deaning as the profession and I have to file away my leanings toward the life of teaching and research. ...So much is lost when we lose touch with those for whom our endeavors are meant to touch, namely, students.

John Piper (Lycoming College)

I came from the faculty—history. One of my conditions in accepting the job was that I teach one course per semester.... As for research, I left two unfinished manuscripts, one needing "simple" revision and one needing about two chapters. I have made little progress.... I believe in the model of the dean on loan from the faculty.... My role is to hire, evaluate, mentor, fire, etc., teachers (professors). I am not sure there is a substitute for experience in the classroom and with colleagues to prepare to do this.

Peter Facione (Santa Clara University)

...I've come to see deaning as a profession, one that includes a great deal of teaching—mostly of chairs and sometimes of faculty. But it is a profession that derives from the faculty role and should remain attached to its roots.

Peter Alexander (St. Peter's College)

My personal preference is for the "faculty member on special assignment" model, but our assistant vice president insists on the "deaning as a profession" model, and you can well guess who wins this debate!... Preferences aside, I find myself constrained by the circumstances of having 23 departments and programs reporting to me—a circumstance which leads me to spend about 55 hours per week in my office and which leaves little time for scholarly activity.

Ronald Dotterer (Salisbury State University)

If you are going to be an administrator, you need to want to, and not be apologetic for your managerial abilities or your capacity to balance a budget or set a strategic goal and get there.... I think it is very important to understand the context in which you will work as an administrator and to be very frank about the leadership styles of those who head an institution, whether they are compatible with your own, and what the decision making processes are on the campus where you are planning to work.

Bari Watkins (Morningside College)

Serving on the faculty is necessary training to be a dean. But that's not at all the same as believing that all deans should or will go back to teaching as the "on loan" model suggests.

David Hoekema (Calvin College)

I don't think there's any general answer to whether to think of administration as a separate profession or a stage in the life of a disciplinary vocation.... But since the question was how to advise a prospective administrator, I have to give credit to my University of Delaware dean, Mary Richards, for some of the sagest advice dispensed to me when I was considering Calvin's offer. "It's a wonderful opportunity, David, and of course you should do it," she advised. "But do keep in mind that none of the problems that you have to deal with have solutions. All the problems that have solutions are fixed long before they get to you. You get all the ones for which there isn't any possible solution."

Relations With Other Deans

Lisa A. Rossbacher, Southern Polytechnic State University

A faculty member at a large, private university in California recently observed that "the dean of his academic division was so bad that even the other deans were starting to notice." In contrast to this particular view of deans being slow to recognize incompetence (and perhaps slower still to criticize), most deans are quick to see problems and identify solutions. Fellow deans can help you by providing perspective, giving advice, and warning you about strategies that might—and might not—work. Developing relationships with deans at other institutions, particularly those with similar missions and sizes, can be an invaluable support.

Some regional consortia have regular meetings of the deans; the Central Pennsylvania Consortium (Dickinson, Franklin and Marshall, and Gettysburg Colleges) is one example of this. Other, larger, groups meet less frequently: a dozen schools in the northeastern U.S. have annual meetings of the academic deans. State university systems sometimes have regular gatherings of deans of colleges and schools with similar interests (arts, science, education, etc.). Some schools use their membership in a particular athletic conference as a mechanism for gathering the academic deans. And some deans have informal lunches or dinners with colleagues who live or work nearby to talk about the issues they are facing.

Several national organizations support the work of deans and the development of collegial relationships among deans. One of these is ACAD, an organization that meets annually in conjunction with the Association of American Colleges and Universities. Another such group is sponsored by the Council of Independent Colleges (CIC). Both groups sponsor workshops for new deans as well.

Electronic relationships with other deans can also be helpful. Two electronic discussion groups, in particular, are focused on the issues facing academic deans. The

ACAD "Deans' List" has about 300 deans who participate in discussions about a wide variety of issues ranging from personnel procedures to faculty development to specific advice for new deans (this handbook is an outgrowth of the discussions on this listserve). The CIC also sponsors a similar list with several hundred members. Although these opportunities are publicized to the members of these organizations, they are currently available to all interested deans. These lists are an excellent way to learn about what other schools are doing, what solutions other deans have found to problems that you share, and what variety exists in the challenges that face institutions. A further benefit of these electronic discussion groups is in finding colleagues who have wrestled with particular issues; following up with a phone call directly to someone who has posted an interesting idea on an electronic list can be very helpful. For more information about the ACAD "Deans' List," send a query to reilly@aacu.nw.dc.us. For more information about the CIC list, contact the CIC office at (202) 466-7230.

Something about which deans rarely speak, but which underlies their professional relationships, is the expectation of confidentiality. In the process of sharing information, deans sometimes reveal sensitive data about their institutions. The code of honor among deans is that this information is never used against another institution. You should never, for example, publicize enrollment drops at a neighboring institution, or share faculty salaries without permission. With permission, however, information from other colleges can be very helpful in illustrating a point on your campus. In situations where institutions compete on the athletic field and for students and faculty, the spirit of competition can threaten to spill over into the relationships between academic administrators. You should resist this vigorously, in the interest of helping everyone do the best job he or she can.

Relationships with fellow deans can also be helpful in preserving your mental health. This aspect of the relationship is more personal and social than professional, but it can be very important. With colleague deans, you can laugh about situations that would befuddle or offend someone who did not deal with them daily. You can learn about time management and stress management. You can find people whose ideas and ethics you admire.

As you develop relationships with other deans, you can also find mentors, although such a discovery is usually a fortunate combination of timing, chemistry, and luck, rather than part of a premeditated plan. Josef Martin (a pseudonym) wrote in his book *To Rise Above Principle: The Memoirs of an Unreconstructed Dean* (University of Illinois Press, 1988): "I'm not entirely alone in believing that mentoring is what learners do for themselves by observing and by thinking, not what anyone else can do for someone who wants to learn." How you can learn, however, includes talking with, observing, and thinking through issues with other deans who face challenges similar to our own.

WHAT TO READ

Samuel M. Hines, Jr., College of Charleston

What dozen books should a person newly appointed to an academic administration position read before assuming office? Answer: read the best current work in your discipline. It's very easy to get out of touch, and very helpful for your sanity as well as your intellectual cardiovascular fitness to know what is going on. Be highly selective, but keep reading.

For every book on management, academic or otherwise, follow immediately with an antidote of real writing, such as good fiction, classic or contemporary. Of course it's impossible to find the time, but find it anyway. One dean finds books on tape from the public library a valuable adjunct to an hour at the gym, both to improve the mind and to drown out the offensive garbage music the gym provides. This dean thinks he/she set a record last year for successive renewals of one set of tapes (the whole of the *Divine Comedy*) and will set another one this year by the time *Anna Karenina* is finished.

There are some publishers who have particularly strong lists in higher education. The offerings are uneven to be sure, but they are constantly adding titles to their lists. It is worth checking their lists regularly. Jossey-Bass, ACE/Macmillan/Oryx, Johns Hopkins, and Anker Publishers are among the best. Of course, some of the publications of the higher education associations are excellent.

If you are going to be the new dean at a school new to you, read the history of the college you are about to serve. I was fortunate to have two such histories to read (one published in 1959 and one in 1980) which were a great help in getting a sense of the place.

Whatever you read, you need to take care not to let your reading be shaped by the false and dangerous idea that there is such a thing in the field as professional expertise, techniques that someone could be taught. But here are some suggestions anyway—from various deans. Most of the annotations are mine.

Administration, Management

Below, Patrick J., George L. Morrisey, Betty L. Acomb. *The Executive Guide to Strategic Planning* (San Francisco: Jossey-Bass, 1987).

> Useful overview of all aspects of strategic planning. If you're a new dean and want to introduce strategic as well as routine planning processes in your college, this would be of real value.

Berquist, William H. *The Four Cultures of the Academy* (San Francisco: Jossey-Bass, 1992).

> One of the best ways for a dean to get into the increasingly vast literature on organization culture. Can be used to stimulate useful discussions with chairs.

Bogue, E. Grady. *Leadership by Design; Strengthening Integrity in Higher Education* (San Francisco: Jossey-Bass, 1994).

> Perhaps a summary of the book's chapter titles will show what weighty—and important—areas he traffics in: The Call of Honor, The Dignity Test, The Habit of Curiosity, The Case for Candor, The Touch of Compassion, The Question of Courage, The Expectation of Excellence, The Servant Exemplar. Thus, Bogue presents a leader (dean, provost) as someone who is characterized as a person of honor, dignity, candor, and compassion. The dean is a person who has both courage and

curiosity and who is motivated by excellence. Most importantly to Bogue, the dean is a person who realizes that to lead one must see himself as a servant. It is well worth reading.

Gibson, Gerald W. *Good Start—A Guidebook for New Faculty in Liberal Arts Colleges* (Bolton, MA: Anker Publishing, 1992).

> An excellent book on faculty development and academic culture in the liberal arts college. A must read for new faculty in those institutions.

Parkinson, C. Northcote. *Parkinson's Law and Other Studies in Administration* (Boston: Houghton Mifflin, 1957).

> The classic commentary on the problems of bureaucratic red-tape and bungling. Still useful reading for anyone in administration. Good source of humorous anecdotes.

Roberts, Wess. *Leadership Secrets of Attila the Hun* (New York: Warner Books, 1985).

> This sounds terrible, but it is very cleverly done and for the careful reader, it is replete with important lessons. Also a source of humorous examples; it is both playful and deadly serious!

Seldin, Peter. *How Administrators Can Improve Teaching* (San Francisco: Jossey-Bass, 1990).

> Lots of excellent ideas here for deans and chairs about how to make your verbal commitment to the primacy of teaching a reality in practice.

Tucker, Allan, *Chairing the Academic Department*, 3rd edition (Phoenix, AZ: ACE/Oryx Press, 1993).

> This has been the standard work on the department chair position and the newest edition is a complete treatment of the subject.

Tucker, Allan, and Robert A. Bryan. *The Academic Dean: Dove, Dragon, and Diplomat* (New York: ACE/MacMillan, 1988).

> I have found this book useful—and entertaining.

Walker, Donald E. *The Effective Administrator: A Practical Approach to Problem Solving, Decision Making, and Campus Leadership* (San Francisco: Jossey Bass, 1986).

> Walker's approach is common sensical and humorous; his pithy one-liners also show an understanding of the breadth of the field and adequate humility.

Wheatley, Margaret J. *Leadership and the New Science: Learning about Organization from an Orderly Universe* (San Francisco: Berrett-Koehler Publishers, Inc, 1994).

> This is a very different sort of management treatise—if you are interested in complexity, chaos, and self-organizing systems, it provides a very readable treatment of these newest developments in science and chaos theory. Good bibliography.

Wren, J. Thomas, ed. *The Leader's Companion: Insights on Leadership Through the Ages* (New York: The Free Press, 1995).

> This new collection of over 500 pages contains some real classics that bear re-reading as well as lots

of up-to-date items. Range of topics related to leadership is broad. Good indexes and list of references. I'm using it in my graduate MPA course on Leadership and Decision Making.

Higher Education

Elster, John. *Choices Over Time* (New York: Russell Sage Foundation, 1992).

> This author's exploration of the nature of rationality in a series of books is among the most original and challenging. See also: *Sour Grapes: Studies in the Subversion of Rationality* (Cambridge: Cambridge University Press, 1983) and *Ulysses and the Sirens: Studies in Rationality and Irrationality* (Cambridge: Cambridge University Press, 1979).

Kimball, Bruce. *Orators and Philosophers* (expanded ed: College Board: 1995).

> A history of the liberal arts in the West from the ancient Greeks to the present, told in terms of iterated versions of the tension between teaching (orators) and research (philosophers).

Newman, Henry. *The Idea of a University* (Oxford, England: The Clarendon Press, 1976).

> The most famous of the defenses of education as the cultivation of intelligent judgment, and the college/ university as needing an ethical (indeed, a religious) foundation.

Oakley, Francis. *Community of Learning: The American College and the Liberal Arts Tradition* (Oxford, England: Oxford Univeristy Press, 1992).

This is not a "how-to" primer for deans but rather a broadly historical and deeply thoughtful assessment of the purposes of higher education in light of current concerns about "curricular coherence, multiculturalism, and the alleged politicization of undergraduate studies."

Pelikan, Jaroslav. *The Idea of the University* (New Haven: Yale University Press, 1992).

An update of Cardinal Newman's classic of the same title, this erudite book is a testimonial to the traditional values of the university.

Taylor, Charles. *Multiculturalism and The Politics of Recognition* (Princeton: Princeton University Press, 1992).

This small volume contains an important essay by the renowned Hegel scholar, Charles Taylor, entitled The Politics of Recognition, followed by commentaries. Much has been written about multiculturalism, but this sophisticated analysis of the politics of recognition is, for my money, the best piece I've read. The intro by Amy Guttman is also excellent.

Whitehead, Alfred North. *The Aims of Education* (New York: Macmillan Co, 1949).

The locus classicus for most quotes about "the nature of education." Essays written 1913-1927 about British education, but they usually sound as though they were written last week in response to last month's higher education controversy.

Serial Publications

Academe Today [on line]
Change
Chronicle of Higher Education
Educational Record
Liberal Studies
Lingua Franca
ASHE-ERIC Higher Education Research Reports
Metropolitan Universities: An International Forum

One of the interesting newcomers is the journal published by the Coalition of Urban and Metropolitan Universities. They've had some interesting special issues.

Classics

Aurelius, Marcus. *Meditations*
Machiavelli, Nicolo. *The Prince*
Sun Tzu, *the Art of War*
Tao Te Ching ("Governing the empire is like cooking a small fish").

Good Novels and Entertainments

Brace, Gerald. *The Department* (Chicago: University of Chicago Press, 1968).

A humane rendering of the teaching, administrating, and scholarly life at a large private university near Boston (not Harvard). Simply to appreciate the level of sensitivity of the first-person narrator would be reason enough for most new deans to read this text.

Kluge, P.F. *Alma Mater: A College Home-coming* (Reading, MA: Addison-Wesley Publishing Company, 1993).

This book affords a wonderful look at Kenyon College by an alum who is also a creative writer. I found it delightful and useful in offering perspective on the entire college or university scene. It also has the virtue of being well written (although I can imagine that some folks at Kenyon College were not all that pleased with it).

Lodge, David *Changing Places* (New York: Penguin, 1975)*; Small World* (New York: Penguin, 1984)*; Nice Work* (New York: Penguin, 1988).

A trilogy about the foibles of the academic life.

Smiley, Jane. *Moo* (New York: Fawcett Columbine, 1995).

An unnamed midwestern university suspiciously similar to Smiley's home campus, Iowa State University: "Chairman X of the Horticultural Dept harbors a secret fantasy to kill the dean...."

Reed, Ishmail. *Japanese by Spring* (New York: Penguin, 1993).

A black junior professor at overwhelmingly white Jack London College lusts after tenure and its glorious perks.

Also contributing to this list:

Thomas Trebon (St. Norbert College)

George Allan (Dickinson College)

Managing Stress

Lloyd W. Chapin, Eckerd College

To be an academic dean is inevitably to know stress. You know stress as one seeking to lead—often in the face of inertia, doubt, misunderstanding, or even hostility. You know stress as one called upon to be a mediator—sometimes between administrative and faculty colleagues, sometimes between faculty, sometimes between faculty and students, and sometimes between the campus community and other constituencies—trustees, alumni, parents, and the media. You also know stress as one who must, perhaps more frequently and more painfully than anyone else in the institution, be the bearer of disappointing news—about budgets, about personnel, about programs. And all this within a context in which you are usually oppressed with the sense that there is never enough time to do things well. The academic deanship can be profoundly rewarding—as many of us will gladly testify—but there is definitely a price to pay in terms of stress.

How can you manage the stress? The suggestions that follow do not grow out of deep psychological research or extensive surveys. However, they do grow out of a long career of academic deaning—almost 30 years spread over three institutions—so at least they have stood the test of first-hand, rather intense and prolonged experience.

1. Maintain realistic expectations for your institution and yourself. Bold visions, major changes, fundamental reform—these can be powerful, inspiring motivators, but remember that such things usually become real only gradually, a step-at-a-time. Focus on making progress, not revolution.

2. Recognize and affirm the value of different, even conflicting, points of view. Remind yourself of the value of dialogical, even dialectical, thinking. Even your most persistently hostile critics can provide you with useful information or a fresh perspective.

3. Take your time responding to persons and problems that you find puzzling or irritating. Very often your initial response is not the best one. A night's sleep, a week's wait, a month's delay will often result in clearer understanding and a more productive idea. Remember that anger is never your friend, always your enemy. Those for whom you are "the Dean" count on you to be, at the least, dispassionate.

4. Everyone gets frustrated, and this leads to another piece of advice: find ways to ventilate your passions invisibly. I have given many a ferocious speech and delivered many a devastating putdown to the shaving mirror and the lawn mower. I also share much with my understanding and infinitely discreet wife. To each his own, but you need a sounding board.

5. Engage in significant and clearly different activities that you find personally rewarding. Henry Rosovsky, Harvard's famous dean of faculty, has observed, correctly I think, that one can never shed the mantle of dean—even in the most relaxed, informal settings—but I believe one can find times and places either alone or with friends to do refreshing and pleasant things that do not involve deaning: gardening, golf or tennis, reading for pleasure, listening to music, walking or jogging, volunteer service, church work, traveling, recreational activities with family. Because the intellectual, social, emotional, and time demands of deaning are heavy, it is relatively easy, but ultimately counterproductive, for a dean to become totally absorbed in professional re-

sponsibilities. Do not do it. Take thought and time to cultivate the soul.

6. Carry out your responsibilities with integrity. People count on the dean to be dispassionate; they also count on the dean to deal honestly and straightforwardly, to abide by institutional policies, to be fair and consistent. Aside from the important moral considerations that ought to underlie such conduct, an important key to managing stress is retaining the sense that however misunderstood or criticized, one's actions and decisions will bear up under public scrutiny.

7. Distinguish major long-term objectives from immediate short-term ones, and be sure to make time to work on the former. In a dean's office, the immediate demands of callers, correspondence and committees can drain your time, your intellectual and emotional resources, and your energy. If they do, your frustration and anxiety will grow. Schedule your time, usually with the help of your secretary, so that you can devote thought to conceptualizing, strategizing, and writing that are usually necessary to make progress on those tasks that have major institutional significance. There is nothing quite so satisfying—and calming—as the sense of achievement that comes from completing a major project that has the potential to make a difference for the long term.

8. Even as you make time to pursue long-term objectives, it is also important for your piece of mind not to get too far behind on immediate specific things— responding to queries, sending thank

you notes, monitoring expenditures, reading reports. Managing stress is often a matter of managing your time effectively—balancing the long-term with the short-term.

9. Stay in touch with fellow deans. One of the best stress relievers is realizing that the problems that test your patience, your faith, and your sanity are usually shared by your counterparts elsewhere. Sometimes they can help you come up with solutions, but they are always a source of intelligent sympathy.

3

Curriculum

ACAD
AMERICAN CONFERENCE
OF ACADEMIC DEANS

Curriculum Evaluation: Department Reviews

Peter Alexander, St. Peter's College

Colleges and universities are largely self-governing institutions. In the interest of fulfilling the public trust, it behooves such institutions to re-examine their operations at regular intervals with a view toward adapting to change, optimizing their processes, preparing for the future, and identifying and correcting problems that may exist. Periodic review of the curricula and operations of academic departments is central to institutional self-analysis and generally falls within the purview of the academic dean.

It is essential that you approach any departmental review process as a collegial, collaborative, and constructive process with an emphasis on self-study and forward-looking planning. Faculty may fear that a review is surreptitiously aimed at cutting a department's staff or resources. Setting a clearly positive tone is necessary if you are to avoid defensive responses which may limit the useful outcomes of a review.

Generally, you should arrange for departmental reviews to occur on a cyclical basis, with several departments being reviewed each year. The duration of a full cycle of reviews ranges from 2 years to 10 years at various institutions, with the longer cycles being prevalent. Interdisciplinary programs and honors programs are often included in review cycles, as are support services when these report to the same officer as the instructional departments. The protocol for review may need to be modified in the latter case.

Departmental review generally entails the gathering of a good deal of descriptive information and data. Summaries of faculty teaching and scholarly activities are a standard item. The results of teaching evaluations by current students and of satisfaction surveys from alumni may be included. Data on enrollments, class sizes, credits offered, frequency of offerings also may be included. If at all possible, you should have such data provided by the administration. Relieving faculty of the need to do compilations of data will allow them to focus on the planning aspects of the review process. Additionally, having the review data in a consistent format provided by the administration will facilitate comparison of results across departments.

Figure 1 gives a model for departmental review that reflects the practices at a number of colleges of arts and sciences. In beginning such a process, it is important for you to provide a clear statement of procedures along with a timetable specifying a completion date for each phase of the process. This review protocol should include a specific set of questions to be answered and/or planning objectives to be met by the department. The items for review generally touch upon all or most of the following areas: departmental curriculum, offerings for the core curriculum or general education program, teaching effectiveness, scholarly productivity, advisement, resources available to the department, and the outcomes of the department's programs.

Be sure that the review process includes bringing in one or more external evaluators. Their perspective is essential to a balanced assessment of a department's activities. Various institutions stipulate from one to three consultants for a review. It is often specified that reviewers should be faculty from institutions of similar character. Professional associations may also serve as sources for consultants. External reviewers should receive, in advance of their visit, all of the materials generated in the earlier phase of the review process, including data, descriptive material (both departmental and institutional), and the department's preliminary report. During

the consultant(s) site visit, there should be opportunities to meet with all of the department members, with yourself (and perhaps other administrators), and with a sampling of the department's students. The report of the consultant(s) should be provided both to the department and yourself (and to the administrative officer other than yourself, if there is one, who was responsible for conducting the review).

You should give the department an opportunity to provide a written reaction to the external report, either as an independent document or by way of inclusion in the final report. The final departmental report, the report of the consultant(s), and supporting documents should be lodged with your office and made available to the curriculum committee. In consultation with this committee—or, better, in collaboration with it—you should prepare a constructive response to these submissions. Such a response may include a follow-up meeting with the department, plans for implementation of recommendations in the final report, and establishment of follow-up procedures.

Finally, review processes evolve. After completing a full cycle of reviews, an institution should do a critique of the results, reorganizing the procedures or refocusing the questions for the next cycle.

The questions below were posted to the ACAD e-mail discussion list. What follows the questions are the responses of a few individual academic officers:

What is the best model for conducting periodic departmental curriculum reviews?
   1. Why perform periodic reviews?
   2. How often should reviews occur?

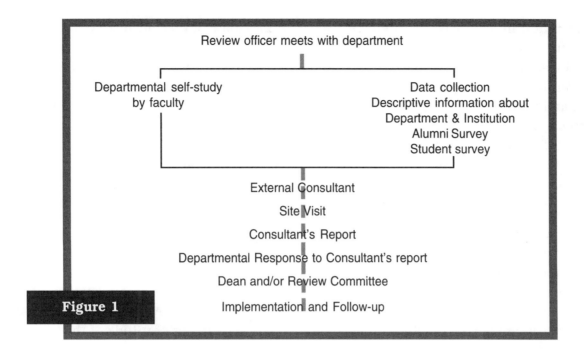

Review officer meets with department

Departmental self-study
by faculty

Data collection
Descriptive information about
Department & Institution
Alumni Survey
Student survey

External Consultant
Site Visit
Consultant's Report
Departmental Response to Consultant's report
Dean and/or Review Committee
Implementation and Follow-up

Figure 1

3. What should be the role in the review of a department played by: the department members, the department chair, the curriculum committee, the dean, the president?

4. Should outside evaluators be used, and if so, how should they be selected and what should be their mandate?

5. What are the key questions to ask in any review?

6. What form should the final results take? Report by whom (outside evaluators, the department)? To whom (curriculum committee, dean/president)?

7. What about formal follow-up procedures?

8. What other factors are crucial (necessary?) to the undertaking, process, and completion of a review?

Keith Boone (Denison University)

We do periodic reviews to make sure departments think through their departmental issues on a regular basis (major and gen. ed. curriculum, support issues, student involvement, etc., but not personnel issues), and so that they get the benefit of feedback from both external and internal reviewers.

The entire department plays a role in writing the self-evaluation, and it is the chair's responsibility to coordinate the self-evaluation. The external team is very important in the process, since they bring a range of perspectives and can supply a comparative perspective. The external team reads the department's self-evaluation and other documents, then visits the campus for two days to conduct interviews with a wide range of people, from the president to faculty to majors to non-majors.

The external team produces a written report within a month after its visit. Then an internal team produces a written report, based on the self-evaluation, external report, and its own interviews. Then the department responds in writing to all the foregoing. Finally, the department chair meets with the president, academic deans, and the chair of the internal review team for a post-mortem and recommendations.

We evaluate three departments a year on a 10-year cycle. We have just finished the first round and will make one major change: elimination of the internal review team. We judged that the costs of this committee, in terms of faculty time and energy—and because of repetition in the process—were not worth the benefits. So now the Academic Affairs Committee will assume the role of an internal reviewer, but in a much truncated way.

The external review team has been made up of one faculty from a liberal arts college similar to Denison, one faculty from a doctoral-granting institution, and one alum who majored in the department. We have found that careful selection of this team—particularly the faculty who chairs it—is critical, both in terms of the ease of the process and the quality of the result.

Karl Reitz (Chapman University)

We do program reviews every six years. In the review we expect the department to assemble a number of statistics (i.e., enrollment patterns, full-time and part-time faculty, their specialties, the number of majors, etc.), address a number of questions, and develop a strategic plan for the next five years. After the department has developed a report with the requisite

information, they invite an outside reviewer to come to campus and spend a day interviewing various groups. The reviewer then writes a report to which the department responds. The whole document then goes to the undergraduate academic committee and/or the graduate committee. These committees have available a number of actions. Mostly they make recommendations to the department and the administration. However, they may mandate certain changes in the program or major including their elimination.

In my opinion, the process has been mostly valuable. A great deal depends on the department's attitude. If they view the review as a chance to review what they have been doing and get a little outside feedback then the process will serve a valuable function. If they view it as an opportunity to congratulate themselves and pressure the administration into giving them more resources, then the process will be somewhat frustrating to the department. In some cases, it has been a very valuable catalyst for positive change.

The main problem that departments have with the process is that they find it difficult to devote the time to doing a good job when they are already over-burdened. In trying to alleviate that difficulty, I have worked at developing a system in which most of the data that they need is gathered for them in a standard format. Then all they need to do is to react to the data and plan for the future. I think this will make the task a little less onerous. We are looking at other ways to make the review a positive experience.

Peter Alexander (Saint Peter's College)

Any curriculum should be reviewed regularly: (a) to be sure it is current, and (b) to check for proper "fit" to the resources embodied in the currently available faculty, and © to see that it continues to meet the needs of students. While most would recognize these or other reasons for review, there is also a tendency to postpone this sort of task, and thus, the need for scheduled periodic review. Ten years ago, we instituted a cyclical academic review process in which every instructional department and program was to be reviewed once every five years with four or five departments evaluated in a given year. At the completion of the first five-year cycle, we modified the process such that we now have a five-year "major" cycle followed by a five-year "minor" cycle. The major cycle entails a great deal of work, requires external evaluators, alumni satisfaction suarveys, and a great deal of both retrospective and prospective evaluation on a large number of criteria. The minor cycle dispenses with external evaluators if there are no pressing problems in a department, and dispenses with alumni surveys, and some other forms of evaluation. The minor cycle emphasizes planning a bit more than retrospective analysis. We have reached the point of completing one major and one minor cycle in 10 years and probably will continue this alternation into the foreseeable future (at least 10 minutes!)

We award a course release to the person in each department who will author the review document and do most of the physical work of retaining evaluators, compiling data, etc. Some departments choose to have the chair do this, while others select another individual,a usually because the chair is overburdened. All members of a department are given the opportunity to contribute to and to review the final document. The dean meets with the department midway through the review to check progress and to offer guidance. The review document is submitted to a review committee, which mainly checks procedure, completeness, etc., and prepares a concise summary in a prescribed format. The report and the summary are then sent to the dean and to the AVP. The Dean, the chair of the review committee, and the AVP confer. The AVP writes the institutional reaction to the review.

As noted above, we require outside evaluators at least once in 10 years, and in problem cases, once in 5 years. We expect evaluators to be senior faculty in parallel departments at similar institutions and mutually agreeable to both the members of the department and the administration. (They also have to be willing to work for the paltry fees we offer!)

The key questions that are addressed in the review are:

1. What courses has the department been offering and how have enrollments fared? Are changes needed because of enrollment trends or because of changes in the discipline or in the faculty roster?
2. What kind and how much scholarly activity has there been? What resources are needed to sustain/enhance this activity?
3. Is the staffing level in the department appropriate?
4. What is the teaching effectiveness of the department?

5. What procedures does the department use to deliver effective advisement to its students. (I hope to strengthen this area of questioning in the next round because some departments seem to have no higher thought than "We answer their questions.")
6. What are the outcomes of the department's offerings, i.e., satisfaction and success of its alumni.

We expect a narrative report incorporating responses to all questions from the department and, separately, from the external evaluator where required. The department may also submit a reaction to the external evaluator's report. Our basic follow-up procedure is as above: report to review committee, report and summary to dean and AVP. The summary in prescribed format prepared by review committee (or actually, by its chair) is very useful because it provides a table that cross-references items in the department's report with external reports and puts things in a constant, streamlined format that allows ready comparison of the results for different departments. After conferring with the dean and committee, the AVP writes the formal institutional response. The single greatest problem in follow up is the possibility of being unable to respond positively to a well-justified call for more resources. When this occurs, as it sometimes must, it has a very chilling effect on the quality of the subsequent review.

The person selected by a department to spearhead a review is *the* crucial factor in determining the success of the process. Choose the wrong person and you'll get a late, incomplete, and shallow report, accompanied by the claim that the outside evaluator "just doesn't understand our

department." The next most crucial factor in long-term success is constructive administrative follow up to the results of the review process.

Paul K. Formo (Dana College)

I will play the contrarian with regard to curricular reviews and suggest that at *some* institutions, periodic review may well be far more counterproductive than productive. If one holds the view, as I do, that curricular reviews ought to be undertaken for the primary purpose of improving what students gain from the program and not just to quantify and compare for the various constituencies that demand it, the process for review must be such that it does that with minimal disruption to the delivery of the curriculum. In very small schools such as Dana College, a formal system which answers the questions above would take more faculty time and more funds to implement than would be productive. If we were to "discover" new funds to support such a venture, I submit that putting them to direct use of departments would be more productive in the long run.

After 12+ years as an academic administrator at three different institutions of various sizes and types, I have noticed that curricular reform is triggered "naturally" by the hiring of new faculty, by periodic accreditation visits (special and regional), and by on-going tinkering to revamping of general education requirements (is anyone ever finished with gen. ed. revision?) so that any other periodic review may well be less necessary for improvement than we think. If there is a need to "downsize," some form of review which gives structure and credibility to the final decisions is necessary. Some would argue, as I used to, that having a formal structure in place before that need arises would be preferable to having to create one under stress. I am now not so sure that the on-going stress of continuous systematic reviews is much, if any, better. I certainly can understand that larger institutions may need to have periodic reviews to accomplish all that is needed. But review for review's sake is questionable at best.

Susan Figge (College of Wooster)

Wooster began a new calendar and format for departmental curricular reviews two years ago. Previously all departments had been reviewed within a two-year time frame. The Educational Policy Committee, chaired by the Dean of the Faculty, now guides three or four reviews each year in a 10-year cycle. We have structured these reviews as an internal self-study, stressing the opportunity they offer departments to address emerging curricular issues, rather than as a process designed for administrators and outside evaluators to make judgments about departmental staffing or other resources.

Central to the self-study are questions formulated by the department and the Educational Policy Committee about the department's goals for student learning in different categories of courses and about the rationale and coherence of its major. Further considerations include the department's curricular connections to other departments, to the college's curriculum as a whole, to graduate and professional school admission requirements, and to general disciplinary trends. As part of the review, departments are expected to invite two external consultants and to

survey alumni of the last 10 years about the role of the major in their subsequent careers.

All members of the department meet with the Educational Policy Committee, the vice president, and the president at the beginning and end of the review process, first to set the agenda for the review and then to follow up on the department's final report. In between these meetings the department carries out its own discussions, surveys alumni, and organizes the consultants' visit. The same process is followed for interdepartmental programs (e.g., Black Studies, International Relations, Women's Studies), each of which has a curriculum committee and some of which have faculty lines.

We are now well into our third year of these curricular reviews and have encountered some unintended, but perhaps predictable, results. In spite of reassurances, departments have worried about the possible use of the review as an evaluation of programs and personnel that could lead to staffing cuts or administrative pressure to restructure the curriculum. In addition, the review has provided an occasion for departments to express accumulated dissatisfactions, and final departmental reports, usually citing the consultants' astonishment that so small a department should be expected to support such a large program, have tended to conclude with pleas for additional staff and reduced teaching loads. Also the consultants' visit has sometimes dominated the review process and become the primary focus of the final report.

While we want to take all departmental expressions of distress seriously, the Educational Policy Committee and I also expect in the future to emphasize more clearly with departments and consultants that the review is not an evaluation by an outside team but rather a self-study, with the consultants serving as advisers to the department during one part of the review process, and that the responses to the self-study, including proposals for curricular revision, should be based on current departmental resources.

At the same time the reviews have clearly given most departments the opportunity to be affirmed, inspired, and challenged by colleagues from beyond the College. Several reviews have been followed by the department's creative curricular redesign efforts, representing new perspectives on the needs and concerns of students, on effective ways to use resources, and on recent changes in disciplinary knowledge and pedagogy. The reviews have brought some departments back into contact with departmental alumni. They have given the Educational Policy Committee a chance to appreciate the scope and rationale of a department's offerings, the nature of its culture, and the talents and activities of its faculty in a context other than personnel decisions, administrative restructuring efforts, or position requests. Each review has yielded useful new questions for subsequent reviews.

In summary I would say that even though the review process is occupying an increasing share of the Educational Policy Committee's work load, it is taking shape as an important tool for departmental curricular renewal and for our long-term curricular planning.

Additional reading on this subject may be found in:

Kells, H.R., *Self-Study Processes: A Guide to Self-Evaluation in Higher Education*, 4th Ed., American Council on Education/Oryx Press, Phoenix, Arizona, 1995.

——, *Program Review and Educational Quality in the Major*, Association of American Colleges, Washington, D.C., 1992.

Curriculum Evaluation: Other Program Reviews

Carol A. Lucey, SUNY College of Technology at Alfred

There are a variety of other agencies that can provide assistance to you as you review your academic programs. In some cases, program accreditation requires periodic review by such agencies. These might include regulatory and oversight entities in some states (e.g., in New York, the State Education Department) or specific curriculum review entities for certain disciplines (e.g., the National League of Nursing (NLN) and the Accreditation Board for Engineering and Technology (ABET)).

Additionally, your own advisory Board for a specific curriculum might be a source of external reviewers. All program reviews, however, should be initiated by the department. The appropriate model for using external support is not unlike the model used by the various regional accrediting agencies such as Middle States and North Central. You start with a period of introspection guided by a departmental committee. This group conducts the review by gathering data necessary to answer a specific set of questions. The committee negotiates a date for a campus visit with the external review team. The complete study of the program, including appropriate appendices of data and survey information, should then be sent to all external reviewers well ahead of the campus visit date.

INFORMATION FOR THE STUDY

The question set which the department review team uses to complete the study ought to be standardized for all your programs to whatever extent that is possible. These questions are generally data-specific. Some questions that usually appear on a program review checkoff list include the following:

❖ Provide enrollment trend data for the last ____ years (generally, since last review). These data should include demographic detail such as the mix of women, minorities, and nontraditional students if diversity is an issue on your campus. Also, if there may have been a change in the level of preparation of incoming students during this time, the demographic data should detail this.

❖ Provide budgetary information for the same time period. Budget information should be broken down into categories such as personnel, supplies and expenses, equipment, contracts, travel, staff development.

❖ Provide data on retention and graduation rates and any other indicators of student success, such as placement of students after graduation.

❖ Provide data, such as survey and focus information on student satisfaction.

❖ Provide updated course information—including outlines, sample syllabi, graded assignments and graded tests—for all required courses and laboratories.

❖ Provide information on teaching faculty, including up-to-date curricula vitae and lists of publications.

❖ Provide detailed information on library holdings, available computer services, and other instructional support services, as appropriate.

❖ Provide up-to-date biographical information on all members of your curriculum advisory group.

CONCERNS WITH EXTERNAL REVIEWS

The following tips should illuminate the process of an external review:

❖ Review teams made up largely of faculty from similar colleges to your own often see their role as supporting their colleagues' need for college resources. When the external team tells you that

you need to add three new faculty to the department and spend more on lab equipment, maintain some healthy skepticism. A more serious conclusion would be one in which a particular area of expertise is mentioned as missing from your staff, or a particular piece of equipment or course outline is labeled as dated.

❖ Your arrangement with the chair of the external review panel should include a specific deadline by which you can expect to receive their report. There should also be an opportunity for you to react to any criticisms. Some agencies permit a private exit session with the review team and the responsible academic officer. Try to arrange this, if possible.

❖ Once the review is complete, make sure to use your results! Use the results of a favorable program review in your college's plan for publicity, development, and enrollment management. Conversely, if a program review includes serious program criticisms, that information should be incorporated into the college's strategic plan. A successful program should address three criteria: 1) relation to the college's mission, 2) quality, and 3) financial viability. The information from your external review should give you insight into (2). If a program is financially viable and fits your college mission, but does not measure up under review, plan to spend some money. If there are quality issues of any kind raised by your review process, and the program also fails to meet your requirements for criteria (1) and (3), you probably need to reallocate resources elsewhere.

Revising the Curriculum

Kathleen Schatzberg, Cape Cod Community College

The ways institutions revise their curricula vary so widely that it is difficult to make detailed recommendations on the procedures that ought to be used. Moreover, these institutional processes are often rooted in historical practice with implicit rather than explicit rules. Yet the process is so fundamental to the success of the institution that as dean you must do whatever is necessary to make it visible, accessible, and routinized. It is essential that the process of curriculum revision be committed to paper in some publication such as a faculty handbook, a procedures manual, or perhaps the bylaws of the faculty senate.

The process must also be efficient. Colleges are notoriously slow to act. Although such measured response often permits critical reflection that supports high quality results, the current pace of change in many fields and disciplines demands that we act quickly to revise curricula or risk losing our students to other institutions that are more rapidly responsive to change. If the process of curriculum revision, from proposal to implementation, takes more than one academic year, the institution should examine and re-design the process, perhaps creating a "fast track" for certain kinds of curriculum revision. If a call for fundamental changes in the process of curriculum revision arises from a single department or division, other faculty may reject it as self-serving. So you must provide leadership in examining the efficiency and effectiveness of the curriculum revision process and in linking changes to the benefits for students and the entire institution.

Changes in a discipline, developments in pedagogy, or the employment field for which students are being prepared may be the most common stimuli for curriculum revision. You need to encourage and support this kind of curriculum revision as frequently as faculty identify a need, although the institutional process should include a means by which faculty are required to demonstrate the validity or urgency of the need. Changes in the discipline most often mean an expansion of the body of knowledge, and the curriculum revision suggested may be to as simple as expanding a three-credit course to four. In responding to what are usually very persuasive arguments in support of expanding a course, you need to remind faculty that every course would be better if it included more material and more hours of instruction. The underlying question that must be answered here is: where in their programs will students take one less credit if this course is expanded? In some institutions, faculty will take each other to task in answering such questions, but in some institutions the dean must play that role.

A second factor that may prompt curriculum revision is a change in enrollment patterns. In these cases, you need to ask some hard questions about whether revising the curriculum represents the most effective response. Other proposals for curriculum revision may arise from the scholarly interests of the faculty. Again, proposals for new electives should he expected to include a plan for how the new courses fit with the overall offerings of the department and the institution.

An explicit cycle of revision on which faculty and administration agree is an exceptionally effective structure because it sets an institutional standard of expectations. The cycle may be tied to institutional accreditation schedules but need not be overly rigid. A typical cycle establishes a calendar by which all programs are due for review every three or four years. However, it should allow for variability by department and for more frequent review when needed. Current technology provides the tools necessary to automate such a process. For example, course outline templates and curriculum revision proposal forms can both be made available in electronic format, a capability that should provide major benefits in efficiency.

The form and elements of the course outline itself may be matters of lengthy institutional tradition, but it is valuable to re-examine them from time to time. Institutions that do not use a standard format with specific elements as a minimum requirement should consider adopting one. It is also useful to distinguish among three levels of course description: the catalogue description, the common course outline, and the syllabus.

The catalogue description typically includes the course prefix and number, its title, the number of credits, the composition of lecture, lab, or other class meetings involved, and a paragraph-long description of the course content. In addition, it includes statements on necessary prerequisites and how frequently the course is offered.

The terms "course outline" and "syllabus" have varying definitions from institution to institution, but I will use the term "common course outline" to mean a description of the course that is more detailed than the catalogue description but describes the course regardless of who teaches it. In this sense, the course outline will include all of the elements of the catalogue description, with the addition of a detailed outline of the content. Institutional sensibilities about the parameters of academic freedom will dictate whether any additional information (such as instructional practices or evaluation methods) should be part of a course outline. The course outline also should include special information such as additional fees, directives on hazardous materials, and so on.

The syllabus, as the term is used here, provides an even more detailed description of the course, including instructor-specific information. Included here would be all of the elements of the course outline, plus the required textbooks and other required or recommended readings; a calendar of assignments, exams, due dates for papers, and so on; statements on the instructor's methods of evaluation, grading procedures and, if relevant, attendance policies, and the instructor's office location, office hours, telephone and fax numbers, and increasingly, e-mail address. Many institutions will also require or suggest a statement of academic integrity that references the institution's policy on academic honesty. A curriculum revision proposal should be accompanied by all the information the curriculum committee will need to evaluate the proposal. It is critical for the author of a proposal (or the author's department) to consult with any other department of the institution that will be affected if *this* proposal is approved. Other elements might include proposed class size, evidence of the need for the revision, an analysis of potential impact on enrollments, details on the need for additional resources or special facilities, and the like.

In many institutions, faculty in a given department take complete responsibility for developing and revising the curriculum. In such cases, your responsibility may be limited to providing for needed resources; insuring that schedules of institutional revision are published and that faculty adhere to them; and communicating proposed changes to other affected departments and approved changes to the offices and staff responsible for recruitment, advising, and publications. In other institutions, the dean plays a substantial role in reviewing, negotiating, and approving curriculum changes. In these institutions, you must seek expert advice or personally commit to acquiring sufficient knowledge of all the fields you supervise to make informed recommendations and decisions. In the case of exceptionally controversial curriculum revision proposals, you may also want to seek advice from external evaluators or consultants.

You should be sure that the flow of curriculum revision proposals is of manageable proportion, but sometimes external mandates or major institutional transformations demand massive, comprehensive curriculum revision. Conversion from a quarter to a semester academic calendar is an example. Although the institution may be able to space a conversion over two, three, or even more years, it is still a revision of such enormous scale that the need for structured timetables and planning cannot be overemphasized. For these kinds of curriculum revision, the advice of institutions that have undergone similar revisions will be invaluable.

These details of curriculum revision may seem routine or even mundane to you. Indeed, this discussion has sidestepped entirely the issue of the territorial and political battles over curriculum for which academia is famous. If there are rules for dealing with these aspects of curriculum revision, they are embedded in the skills of negotiation and mediation, and you would be well-advised to seek professional development opportunities to hone these skills. Let me note also that a curriculum proposal may seem to demand a response of approval or rejection, but another choice is to do nothing, at least for a time. Such a hiatus may provide the context in which opponents find common ground or a seemingly irresolvable conflict finds its resolution.

Most academic administrators are themselves former teachers who found that they possessed certain organizational talents that led them to take on administrative roles. Most of us, at one time or another, pine for the classroom and the immediacy of the teaching-learning moment. That vast body of collective work known as the curriculum, however, forms the very heart of what the institution offers students, and the successful management of its revision can become one of the most satisfying aspects of academic leadership.

Resource Handbook for Academic Deans

The Politics of Change

Charles D. Masiello, Pace University

INTRODUCTION

The world is changing at an ever increasing rate. To be competitive in today's environment, universities must examine how to manage resources, increase productivity, reduce costs, and get work done. Such an analysis almost always results in the realization that change is necessary. But change is also difficult, and the question invariably becomes how to achieve it.

Change is pervasive; indeed, to be alive implies change. Yet anyone who has worked at a university knows that there is probably no other environment that is more resistant to transformation. This should come as no surprise given the long-established, rich, and complex traditions of the academy, where people are trained to be independent thinkers who are reticent to accept insight or direction from others without proof of its value.

There is also the competition among rival interest groups or individuals for power and leadership—politics. Nowhere is it stronger than at a university. So much so that it is said that when Woodrow Wilson left the presidency of Princeton University to enter government in Washington, he commented that he had learned the art of politics from the professionals and was now going to Washington to practice with the amateurs. His wife is reported to have said that she was glad that Woodrow was leaving the world of politics to enter government. Such stories, while amusing, reveal the long recognized difficulties in creating substantive transformation in an academic setting.

How, then, can you help bring about the changes that you view as essential to the well-being of your institution and the furtherance of its mission in an environment where the mere mention of change generates ripples of anxiety and resistance? Volumes have been written on this subject, and detailed resources are readily available. I shall try, in what follows, to provide a brief introduction to the subject with a view toward stimulating discussion.

THREE BASIC RULES

Three simple, but effective, suggestions with which to begin: Listen intently, communicate effectively, and behave ethically.

Listening will enable you to understand the culture or cultures within which you will have to work to bring about the desired results. For our purpose, "listening" also includes doing a substantial amount of institutional analysis, including an assessment of how information is conveyed and how performance is evaluated. Such analyses provide valuable insights and establish a baseline from which to work. Effective communication is a powerful tool. Use it!

Having developed a clear vision of what needs to be accomplished, don't keep it to yourself or assume that people will effortlessly acquire your vision. Communicate it clearly, compellingly, and often. A case for change that is persuasive and clearly articulated will likely be accepted by some, probably after considerable discussion during which much can be learned. These individuals can become allies and sponsors of change.

Finally, be candid and ethical. Besides being the right thing to do, treating people honestly and fairly will engender trust, and trust is essential to gaining the support you will need to implement your vision.

STRATEGIES FOR SUCCESS

Keep in mind that you are the one responsible for nurturing a culture that values and embraces change. This is key to the long-term future success of your institution since continuous creativity and change are essential in the quest for quality and relevance. In the short term, you are responsible for communicating a vision of the future, modifying it based on new insights and feedback that you receive, encouraging teamwork while clarifying lines of authority, setting expectations, establishing principles, policies, and procedures that guide work, and developing accountability standards. These may seem like daunting tasks, but you are assisted in these responsibilities by many others, including faculty and your own staff. Ultimately, however, these items are your responsibility. Remember change or transformation requires an assessment of current conditions, the creation of an effective integrated organizational design, a detailed realizable implementation plan, and a supportive performance measurement system.

Nothing will build confidence in your leadership like success. So if your vision calls for deep, complex, and widespread change that will require substantial time to achieve, consider the following along the way. Identify some easy targets—projects that require no more than a few months to bring to fruition, that do not need large infusions of resources, and that are win-win situations for all. For more complex ventures, introduce pilot projects that are smaller in scope, but nevertheless are part of your integrated plan. Such projects enable you to test the waters by providing valuable feedback and opportunities for modification, increasing the chances of ultimate success. Some pilots may fail; accept that fact and learn from the experience. Finally, if you have a success story, be certain to tell it.

Success usually does not depend on people doing more work, although there may be instances in which this is necessary. More often successful change depends on people doing work differently. Habits die hard, and you may have to expend considerable energy in convincing people to alter their work processes. Consider whether three signatures are really necessary on that authorization form. Would one foster both efficiency and accountability, and at the same time flatten the organization by distributing responsibility and empowering others? Time wasters must be eliminated! People may not be able to do more, but they can do things differently if empowered. Of course, this assumes trust and confidence in those with whom you work. An appropriate performance measurement system can be helpful here. Challenge those who work for and with you to be the best they can be, help them to achieve this mutually beneficial goal, and hold them accountable for it. Remember, however, that job-related training and staff development, appropriate information, and adequate resources are essential to an effective and efficient operation. To do a good job, colleagues need this kind of help and it is your responsibility to provide it.

Be certain also to provide recognition and support for those individuals and teams that function well and establish consequences for those that do not. Encourage continuous learning, creativity, flexibility, and initiative—but always in the context of

accountability and a reward system that makes sense in terms of institutional goals. Make it clear that you expect every person to find ways of cutting costs and improving services, to be willing to take risks, to accept responsibility, to create new ways of working, and to recognize the need for teamwork and continuous personal, unit, and institutional improvement. Be aware of the factors that motivate people to do a good job. These include: interesting work, appreciation/recognition, and being part of a supportive team.

There are many reasons why people do not recognize the need for change. Tunnel vision can prevent them from seeing the significance of events. Also, if they are vested in a situation, they may unconsciously distort information that they receive. If they see themselves as being personally disadvantaged by change, they will likely resist it. Then too, competing cultures, not the least of which are administration and faculty, exist at every institution. Consequently, opinions as to approach will vary widely. Unclear or contested goals also dampen efforts. Such impediments to change should be acknowledged and discussed in an effort to diminish them. Denial of a problem or resistance to change usually signals that a compelling case for change has not been made.

Change is more readily achieved if there is shared understanding among the leadership of a university that substantive alterations are needed for success. Confusion at the top leads to failure. Administrators must identity those items that require change and be clear about expected results. A clear vision of the future is a prerequisite for change. Attention must be paid to making the organization more amenable and responsive to change on an on-going basis. It is essential to develop an organizational culture that values and promotes innovation, initiative, creativity, candid communication, teamwork, and shared decision-making. Accurate and complete data are essential to building consensus on the need for change. Clear identification and communication of problems are extremely important. Many members of the community may not be aware of the problems. Communicate information about problems clearly and directly to all. Remember that change is expedited by building widespread awareness of problems and their underlying causes. Teams can be useful in identifying issues, stimulating creative thinking, and building a united effort. However, teams are not likely to be useful if their members perceive that solutions will endanger their employment. Finally, once the decision to change is made, it must be supported by the entire leadership of the university.

SUMMARY GUIDELINES FOR CHANGE

- ❖ Get the lay of the land by examining current cultures and conditions.
- ❖ Challenge the status quo and encourage change.
- ❖ Foster a culture that values and expects change.
- ❖ Identify problems and determine underlying causes.
- ❖ Communicate problem areas.
- ❖ Establish a baseline grounded in relevant data against which to measure success.
- ❖ Set realistic priorities.

- ❖ Assess your ability to provide needed resources.
- ❖ Develop teams to address the issues.
- ❖ Give clear charges, and keep units on track by asking probing questions.
- ❖ Insist on creative thinking and comprehensive solutions.
- ❖ Articulate a clear vision and an appropriate implementation plan.
- ❖ Establish and communicate measurable goals, operating policies and procedures.
- ❖ Make clear who is in charge.
- ❖ Explain at each stage why things are being done.
- ❖ Realize that ethical behavior and trust are essential.
- ❖ Walk the talk.
- ❖ Start with win-win projects.
- ❖ Use pilot projects to test new waters, to gain insights, and to work out problems.
- ❖ Allow corrections along the way.
- ❖ Provide mechanisms for performance and system appraisal.
- ❖ Insure that expectations and rewards are in sync.
- ❖ Communicate accomplishments so that the beneficial results of change are evident.
- ❖ Celebrate change and positive contributions.
- ❖ View change as presenting opportunities rather than perils.

SOME REACTIONS FROM OTHER DEANS

What would you add to this list developed by Charles Masiello—or subtract from it— or insist on having clarified?

John G. Heilman (Auburn University)

The concept of "change" is used here in the broadest possible sense. The discussion therefore ends up as a list of pointers about management in general. Is management the same as "effecting change?"

You might focus on the kinds of change that should be on the table. One way to do this is to take the first idea, relating to getting the lay of the land, and put it in terms of specifying the area or kind of change one is looking at, identifying stakeholder groups, and finding out where they are with respect to the change "opportunity" at issue.

Bari J. Watkins (Morningside College)

I might add: Use risk-free brainstorming sessions to develop new ideas. Reward even minor efforts to change with praise and personal contact.

Genie Gerdes (Bucknell University)

I like your list but would suggest some additions and one deletion. These arise from my perspective in relation to a faculty that is anything but passive, that abhors top-down administration, and that innovates constantly.

I've added a new #1. Change should be in a direction; I think that there has to be some consensus on that direction. Second, for a faculty like ours, I would change the order of the first elements of the list to avoid the suggestion that change for change's sake is the goal—sometimes our problem is holding to a path we have carefully selected for long enough to see the effect. I'd use this order:

1. Identify institutional priorities and strategic strengths.

2. Get the lay of the land by examining current cultures/conditions.
3. Foster a culture that values and expects change.
4a. Identify problems and determine underlying causes.
5a. Communicate problem areas.
6a. Challenge the status quo and encourage change.

I'd add an alternative path following #3:
4b. Listen well to faculty-initiated suggestions for change.
5b. Be explicit about evaluating those proposed changes in terms of institutional priorities and help the proposers do the reality testing necessary to strengthen the proposal.
6b Support those changes that enhance the priorities in #1, and be perceived as supportive.

Sometimes at Bucknell the administration is perceived as getting in the way of good ideas (of playing the parental role of saying "What if…?" "There isn't enough money" etc.) It's important to convey that truly good ideas (those that advance the priorities) are supported, even if they came from the faculty rather than from us. This b list of supporting or even enhancing grassroots change could be expanded more fully.

Given our faculty's sense of the importance of consensual leadership, I'd also remove your principle, "Make clear who is in charge." The old community organizer approach of stimulating change without having the change attributed to you, and thereby broadening ownership, might be more appropriate for many of our faculties. At Bucknell, most of our committees are a somewhat confusing mix of faculty members and the administrators to whom the committee recommends. Although the administrators often provide information in a way that is very effective in determining the committee directions, the faculty members know they have the ability to influence the relevant administrators and in the end they usually own the decisions and present them to their faculty colleagues. The division of responsibility is not very clear, and for us it works better that way.

Dorothy M. Feigl (Saint Mary's College)

I would challenge the assumption, incorporated in several places on the list, that change per se is a good. Change may be good and necessary, but "Challenge the status quo and encourage change" is too absolute a statement and implies that those arguing for tradition are wrong, period.

I do see the dean as an agent of change and serving in that role to counter academe's strong inclination to the status quo…effectively the dean should be attempting to maintain a healthy, balanced dynamic that recognizes value in both tradition and change. (Which also means that the dean may have to, on occasion, ask the question: where is the evidence that this change will actually benefit students? The new computer-based technologies offer a particular challenge in this regard, not simply because one is often dealing with both Luddites and true-believers, but also because the stakes are so high in terms of the commitment of resources.)

Outcomes Assessment

Lloyd W. Chapin, Eckerd College

One would think that systematically assessing the educational effective ness of academic programs would be a natural part of any college or university's operations, but in fact it is a relatively recent development and is usually implemented reluctantly—at least initially—by most faculties and deans. The reasons for this resistance are the fear that assessment will be used to justify negative personnel decisions, that it will be more costly in time, energy, and money than it is worth, and—the most frequently voiced complaint—that it cannot escape being simplistic, reductionist, and yield insignificant results. Although each of these concerns has some legitimacy, the benefits of outcomes assessment greatly outweigh the risks. The process can induce greater clarity about educational objectives; shed light on curricular strengths and weaknesses; improve teaching; increase the faculty's sense of responsibility for the curriculum as a whole; build credibility with important external constituencies such as parents, funding agencies, and accrediting agencies; and, if undertaken in the right way, be inherently very interesting intellectually.

Keys to the development of a successful outcomes assessment program are:

1. A planning process that is open and widely participatory with faculty having the primary responsibility to formulate policy, program objectives, and assessment strategies.

2. Initial and continuing clarity about the ultimate goal, which is program improvement, not the evaluation of individuals.

3. Starting gradually with projects that can be completed quickly and yield interesting, usable information.

4. Not trying to assess everything at once and all the time, but rather establishing a schedule in which each program comes up for review every three to five years.

5. Clarity about the scope of the assessment effort. For academic deans this typically means a system that includes reviewing the various components of the academic program and possibly the various aspects of student services that contribute directly to student learning.

6. Identifying measurable educational objectives (that is, student learning outcomes) for each academic program to be assessed, for example, measurable competencies for majors and general education; measurable developmental objectives for student affairs.

7. The inclusion of external means of evaluation, for example standardized tests, questionnaires, evaluators from outside the institution. (Grades given to students do *not* constitute outcomes assessment).

8. Policies insuring the accuracy, and the appropriate retention of data.

9. Identifying to whom, and in what formats, data and their interpretations are to be reported, and providing an opportunity for the participants in programs being assessed to review the data before they are passed on to a third party.

10. Providing adequate and competent staff support. The person(s) operationally responsible for gathering and interpreting data should enjoy high credibility with the faculty.

11. "Closing the loop," that is to say, being sure that there is a clearly defined process for using the results of outcomes assessment to improve the academic program. This usually involves a faculty committee with responsibility for curriculum development reviewing the assessment reports and making recommendations as appropriate.

THE ACCREDITATION SELF-STUDY

Walter C. Swap, Tufts University

This is not meant to be an all-inclusive guide to accreditation. Rather, I offer what I hope will be helpful suggestions for preparing for and carrying out the self-study that leads up to accreditation.

All accrediting agencies require a self-study. All include standards, although these may vary from agency to agency. Colleges and universities beginning the process may elect a minimalist approach, dealing directly with each of the standards; or they may decide to use the accreditation process as an opportunity to develop full strategic plans for the future. This often means going beyond the required standards and developing one's own. Finally, if the institution has recently completed an extensive strategic plan, this can often be used as the basis for the self-study. Most accrediting Boards will welcome the opportunity to discuss this with you.

You will be informed about two years in advance that you will be visited. Before that, you can always write to get the standards. (The Southern accrediting agency, for one, is on the web.) The accrediting agency will send you a list of what it wants

Here, now, are the "helpful hints."

1. The president needs to acknowledge that the accreditation process is important, and should urge those who will actually be doing the work for accreditation that the institution should do a good job. Top-down encouragement is important.

2. The person charged with shepherding the process should be *very* well organized. At Tufts, the director of Institutional Planning, who was used to dealing with large databases, did a great job. The "shepherd" needs to construct a timetable, working backwards from the future site visit to the present, a two-year interval! Remember always to overestimate the amount

of time each step in the process will take!

3. Unless the minimalist approach is being used, you will need wide buy-in and involvement from the entire community. This begins with the formation of a steering committee of appropriate administrators and faculty who span the different areas of the institution. The steering committee appoints the committees that will write the reports for each standard, and reads and edits these reports.

4. The committees formed for each standard should have a chair who is reliable and attentive to details. The "shepherd" must rely on the chairs to meet deadlines and to respond to criticisms. An ideal committee will be composed of administrators and faculty and, when appropriate, students, staff, alumni, and trustees. Each group will need clerical support, and this must be budgeted. If possible, the "shepherd" should arrange for someone from his or her staff to be on each committee, to serve as an informal liaison. Committees should be encouraged to hold open hearings to listen to the concerns of university constituents.

5. There will be a page limit (e.g., 100 single-spaced pages in the Northeast), so committees need to stay within fairly rigid limits (depending on how many committees there are). Stagger the dates when the committee reports need to be submitted to the steering committee, with the more straightforward ones due first. Insist on electronic versions in a consistent word processing program. Naturally, there should be backup copies.

6. A great deal of supplementary materials will be required: faculty CVs, course syllabi, course catalogs, etc. Someone must be given the responsibility for collecting all of these from departments and administrative offices.

7. Be sure to leave sufficient time to edit the final version, about three months from receipt of committee reports to the final draft. Consider hiring a professional editor to create the proverbial "seamless document."

8. When the final, edited draft is complete, send a copy to each committee to review for accuracy. This should be done no less than one month prior to the date for the final report. The self-study should be mailed six weeks before the site visit.

9. Rooms that will be required by the visiting team should be booked very early. Taking no chances, we reserved the most popular rooms 2 years in advance. You will need to have a work room, complete with computer, telephone, and office supplies. Arrange for file cabinets to be installed to house the materials. The work room needs to be secure, with good locks. This room, or one adjacent to it, will house the various supplementary materials and documents.

10. Travel arrangements need to be made well in advance. (Your institution pays for these.) The chair of the team will probably need a suite for meeting space. Visit the hotel to ensure it is appropriate. If your institution has more than one campus, you will need to arrange shuttle service. Office supplies should be waiting for the team at

the hotel. Check on any dietary restrictions.

11. Inform everybody at your institution whom the team might want to meet to keep their schedules as open as possible during the visit. It would be embarrassing if the very professor they most want to see is out of town.

12. If you are going to have any open meetings (or if the team requests one or more), don't rely on people's intrinsic interest and desire to talk. Recruit a sufficient number of faculty, students, etc. to ensure a good audience.

13. Develop a matrix of where each team member will be at all times, with telephone numbers or office extensions. The shepherd should have a cellular phone at all times.

14. Have a really big party and congratulate yourselves on a job well done and another 10 years of accreditation.

Curriculum

4

Personnel

ACAD

AMERICAN CONFERENCE
OF ACADEMIC DEANS

HIRING NEW FACULTY

Linda H. Mantel, Willamette University

Participation in the hiring of new faculty is one of your most important responsibilities, one in which your legacy to the institution as dean will be most visible. Depending upon the custom and governance of your college or university, you will either have a significant voice in this process or will have near-final decision-making authority. The outline below suggests the important steps you should take in order to bring about a successful search for a tenure-track position.

SETTING UP A SEARCH

Normally, when you have authorized a replacement or an additional position for a department or a program, the department involved prepares a draft of a position description. A search committee is then appointed, through the normal governance process, and this committee hones the description into its final form as an advertisement. Before the position is advertised, you should approve the ad. The ad is then placed in one or a number of appropriate outlets, nowadays this includes both print and electronic media. In addition, if the position is in any way unusual by virtue of field or level of expertise sought, the chair of the committee will often contact colleagues at other institutions to assure that a wide net is cast.

If support for searches is housed in the Dean's Office, this process will include acknowledgment of receipt of applications and letters, maintaining files, arranging for interviews at meetings, and organizing on-campus visits. If the institution practices affirmative action, records may need to be kept of the nature of the applicant pool. When the search is completed, candidates should receive a letter informing them of the outcome of the search.

Since a dean normally interviews all candidates who are invited to campus, it is useful for you to meet with the search committee as soon as the process begins and before the closing date for the ad. It is important that you have a clear idea of what the search committee is seeking. What are the characteristics of each candidate that will weigh heavily in the committee's recommendations to the dean? Here are some useful questions to address these issues:

1. What will be the role of this new person in the curriculum of the department or program? If the person is a replacement for another colleague, does the department want the same expertise? If it is a new position, what will it add to the program? With whom outside the department will the new colleague be expected to interact? Will they need to take part in an interdisciplinary course or program?

2. What are the most important characteristics of applicants that make them into candidates? How important is a completed Ph.D.? How important is solo teaching experience? What about post-doctoral research? Does a candidate need to have a book in press or published? Is experience in a large or in a small school an advantage or a disadvantage?

3. Are there any problematic aspects to this search? Are there inside candidates, perhaps visiting faculty? How will they be treated with respect to interviews at national meetings and on campus? Is it likely that the pool will be unusually large or unusually small?

4. Who reads the files? How many readers determine whether an applicant becomes a candidate? At what point do outsiders (that is, faculty who are not part of the department) read files?

Discussion of these questions with the entire committee is useful not only for you, but also for participating faculty members and students who may not have been a part of the departmental decision-making process. It is also important, at the first meeting of the search committee, to review AA/EO guidelines, making sure the committee is clear about avoiding illegal questions, and that the committee chair knows how to document the search properly.

SELECTING THE CANDIDATES

Once the applicant pool has been winnowed down to a preliminary list, faculty will often interview 12-20 candidates at a national meeting. If committee members do not plan to attend such a meeting, it is recommended strongly that they contact several references for each person by telephone before preparing a short list, and that they also talk to the candidates. Telephone interviews can be effective at this stage of the search. These screening processes usually result in a list of 5 to 10 candidates who look most promising. You should meet with the chair of the committee again at this point to look over the files to insure that the pool is as broad and deep as possible, and that the committee's judgement on the top candidates is justified. Normally, three or four candidates are invited to campus for a visit.

For those institutions seeking to increase the diversity of faculty, searches that include candidates from under-represented minorities in the field are important. The normal institutional search process will often fail to include such persons. For instance, if the only applicants deemed worthy of candidacy come from Princeton, Yale, Chicago, or Columbia, the pool is unlikely to be diverse. The number of under-represented minorities is small in some fields and more sizeable in others. A knowledge of the field, of the graduate programs that attract under-represented students, and of the faculty who train them, is essential in order to find suitable applicants who can then become candidates. Personal contact through a good network is the most efficacious way to hear about such candidates. Faculty (and deans) attending national meetings should keep their antennae out for promising young scholars.

MAKING THE APPOINTMENT

A dean usually is allotted 45 to 60 minutes to meet with each candidate. Often a breakfast is a convenient time to meet. You should reread the candidate's file and review what was learned at the meeting with the search committee. The interview should provide a sense of the candidate as a teacher, a scholar, and a person; what their academic goals are, how they interact with students, what they enjoy about their work, how they relate to their professional field. You might talk about the advantages and disadvantages of large and small schools; about the institution's culture and ethos; and about the expectations that students and faculty have for themselves and each other. How will the candidate fit into the institution? Except in fields close to your own, faculty should be the judge of the candidate's scholarship.

When all the interviews for a particular search have been completed, you might wish to send a letter or speak to the chair of the committee, providing your assessment of the candidates. The search committee will review information from faculty and students and prepare a recommendation for the appointments committee and yourself.

Regardless of an institution's governance procedure in terms of deciding upon a candidate to be offered a position, you will normally play a central role in determining the initial rank and salary and the availability of funds for start-up. Depending upon the institution's practice, starting salaries may be set college-wide or negotiable according to particular disciplines. A useful carrot for ABD's is to make an offer in the spring at a given rank (Instructor) and salary level and let the candidate know that if the degree is completed before the start of the school year, he or she will immediately be advanced to a higher rank (assistant professor) and salary level. In most cases, you will have some flexibility in negotiating starting salary. For candidates with post-doctoral experience, a starting salary above the entry level is to be expected. In addition, the tenure clock should be made clear at the time the offer is made, and the schedule for pre-tenure reviews should be outlined.

A generous start-up package often makes the difference between an acceptance and a refusal of an offer. Common start-up items may include computers, renovations of office or laboratory space, office furniture, laboratory equipment, student assistance for scholarship or research. Institutional resources and equity are the prime determinants of an appropriate offer. If a candidate comes with a research grant from another institution, negotiation with the granting agency and the original institution must often be carried out.

A successful search often requires filling the employment needs of two people, the candidate and his/her spouse. Although you are not permitted to ask a candidate about family status, the subject is often brought up by the candidate during the interview or at another time during the search visit. In general, the more you know about factors impinging upon a desirable candidate, the more realistic the offer you can make. Knowledge of the academic and professional market in the area can be very helpful in providing leads

and contacts for the spouse of a candidate. Conversely, if an attractive arrangement for a spouse accompanies a competing offer and yours does not, you may lose the candidate.

SUMMARY

A successful tenure-track search requires careful thought, planning, stock-taking, and feedback among yourself, the faculty, and the candidates throughout the process. Surprises should be minimized. Both the candidate and the institution should have a clear idea of each other's expectations, and the successful candidate should be prepared to meet these expectations from the beginning of the appointment.

Evaluating Probationary Faculty

Linda H. Mantel, Willamette University

THE PROCESS

Evaluation of new faculty before tenure is a complex process, requiring the attention of faculty colleagues in the candidate's department, those outside the department who interact with the candidate, students, and yourself as dean.

A candidate who begins a teaching career without significant post-doctoral research or independent teaching experience usually has a probationary period of five or six years, with permanent tenure beginning the sixth or seventh year. Institutions are highly variable with respect to the frequency of pre-tenure evaluations, with significant processes occurring yearly, every other year, or only once before tenure. One important role you can play during the hiring process is to discuss with the candidate how long the tenure clock will be, based on his or her prior experience, and when evaluations will occur during that time.

In those cases where faculty are included in a bargaining unit, the contract may stipulate frequency of evaluation, topics to be covered, and methods of providing feedback to the faculty member. The role of the department chair and the dean in the process of evaluation and reporting may also be stipulated.

One way to oversee faculty development before tenure is to appoint a two- or three-person consultative committee for each new faculty member. This committee will be responsible for observing the teaching of their candidate, for providing specific feedback on teaching visits, and for meeting each year with the candidate to summarize and comment on activities in the areas of teaching, scholarship, and service.

Depending upon the governance structure of the institution, various faculty bodies and the dean normally review candidates before tenure. At the end of the process, you should provide a written summary of the review to the candidate, with a statement in writing that includes descriptions of the candidate's strengths and weaknesses, along with suggestions for improvement. These can be useful documents for charting progress over the years until the time of tenure. Be sure a copy of your summary goes to the faculty member's department chair and that a copy is put in a personnel file that will be available to the various groups that will play a role in subsequent evaluations.

CRITERIA OF EVALUATION

Orientation of new faculty should include a presentation by yourself, perhaps with the assistance of the faculty chair of the tenure and evaluation committee, on the timing and criteria for evaluation and advancement. Some important topics to cover include the following: What does this institution believe to be most important? Will there be formal evaluation of teaching by students? by other faculty? by the department chair? What are the expectations for scholarship in the early years of an appointment? What will the teaching expectations be? How can a new faculty member receive assistance with teaching or scholarship? Is committee work expected? How important is advising students?

If a faculty member's responsibilities are likely to increase for the second year (e.g., by the addition of committee work or advising), it is useful for you to have another session for new faculty at the end of the first year, to prepare them for their new responsibilities and to review the evaluation process. By this time, they will have a framework within which to ask questions,

and they will be better able to focus on these topics than they were during the blur of faculty orientation.

Peer evaluation of teaching is a necessary component of faculty development. There are many possible models by which new faculty can exchange class visits with more senior colleagues. The more such visits are routine, the better the information to be gained. As stated above, immediate and thorough feedback on teaching, with examples of problems and suggestions for improvement, makes the system worthwhile. Inclusion of syllabi in the evaluation file provides the opportunity for faculty colleagues who have not observed the candidate to make some judgements on the quality of the course being taught.

Student evaluation of teaching, by means of questionnaires and solicitation of letters, is the norm in most institutions. The weight that these evaluations carry is highly variable, particularly over the career of the faculty member. All deans tell stories of irate parents saying about a senior faculty member: "How can you let that person continue to teach?" A useful questionnaire will take into account the variety of students enrolled in the course and the role of the course in their program. Frequent review of the contents of the questionnaire by an appropriate faculty body will help to provide a level of comfort in its use.

Letters from students, particularly those who have been academic advisees or who have done independent study with the faculty member, are also important additions to the teaching portfolio.

Institutions and departments vary in their expectation for scholarship and service. Candidates for tenure-track positions often ask whether they need to "have a book" or "get an NSF grant" in order to be considered favorably for tenure. You and the department chair should be as forthright as possible in answering these questions. This will provide junior faculty with a good idea of where to focus their time—on teaching, on developing new syllabi, on scholarship or lab research, on joining committees. They should not be expected to do everything at the same level of intensity, and careful direction can help to prevent burnout.

81

Personnel

Evaluating and Compensating Tenured Faculty

David E. Leary, University of Richmond

Before discussing the evaluation of tenured faculty and the issue of merit-based salary increases, there are a few common-sense principles to keep in mind: (1) every academic community has its own history, priorities, and practices; (2) there is no single way to do anything; and (3) something may work well in one community and cause terrible havoc in another.

With these caveats, it is still difficult to imagine an academic community that does not need and could not profit from some kind of regular faculty evaluation process, even for tenured faculty. Furthermore, although it is somewhat easier to imagine a community that might not wish to have superior performance rewarded by merit-based salary increases, I will assume that most communities, on the principle of fairness, would want to offer some form of recognition for superior performance, whether or not such performance is judged on a group or individual basis.

Practices regarding the review of tenured faculty seem to fall into three distinct categories:

1. *Annual Review.* The rationale for an annual review process is that the performance of all faculty, whether tenured or not, should be reviewed each year with an eye to incremental year-to-year improvement. Even though fundamental change may take place over longer periods of time, annual reviews provide an opportunity for encouraging, fine-tuning, and keeping the faculty member, the chairperson, and yourself aware of ongoing aspirations and achievements as well as current obstacles and needs. Although an annual review (like any review) can be a negative experience for some faculty, ideally it should keep the individual focused on tangible development and help those responsible for salary increases recognize and reward actual, documented accomplishments rather

than reward reputations based on past performance, whether good or bad.

2. *Periodic Review.* The rationale for a process involving less frequent (but regularly scheduled) reviews for tenured faculty—for instance, a review every second, third, or fifth year—is that tenured faculty have proven their basic capabilities and their ability to fulfill their basic responsibilities, and they will now grow and perform better if they are given greater latitude in terms of reporting and oversight. In larger institutions, it may also be the case that the cost of annual reviews (in terms of the faculty member's, chairperson's, and dean's time) is perceived to exceed the probable benefit. Although the underlying purpose of periodic reviews is the same as for annual reviews, the unit of analysis is larger, thus allowing for natural fluctuations of annual teaching, scholarship, and service "outcomes." Generally, in a periodic review system, the expected rate of annual salary increase is determined each time the tenured faculty member is reviewed, though there are sometimes opportunities for modification if some significant change occurs between reviews.

3. *Crisis Review.* The rationale for a crisis review (sometimes called a "post-tenure review") is that a faculty member should be subjected to careful, thorough scrutiny if his/her performance has been found or is suspected to have fallen below an acceptable level for an appreciable period of time. Such reviews may result in a demand for some specific kinds of improvement over one, two, or three years. Generally, there is a mandated follow-up review at the end of this period, and in some institutions, a second unsatisfactory review of this sort may result in the loss of tenure and position. Although this kind of review may take place in an institution that has an annual or periodic review process, it is listed here as a separate type because it may also occur within institutions that do not have a regular faculty evaluation process. Frankly, it is difficult to understand how a system without regular annual or periodic reviews is beneficial to faculty, much less to their students and their larger academic community. If annual or periodic reviews are taken seriously by all parties, the need for crisis reviews as a means of amelioration or termination should be rare.

Good arguments may be made for either annual or periodic reviews, and as noted at the start, the "right" approach for any given institution must be determined in relation to its own local culture and situation. However, looking at evaluation as a necessary and useful part of the larger process of faculty development, it seems reasonable to conclude that each institution should review faculty performance as often as it is practicable to do so, given the other demands upon all those involved. There is no reason that an annual review cannot take into account the longer period of time that is needed for significant change and accomplishments, nor should it be impossible for chairpersons and deans to modulate judgments about a single year within the context of a longer period of time. However, if reviews are done less frequently than each year, chairpersons and deans should be certain to stay in touch with faculty, both to know how they are doing and to offer encouragement and other forms of support. As persons and professionals, faculty tend to care as much about attention and praise as about salaries and being left to their own devices.

The question of merit pay increases is complicated, and there are many variants in how merit pay is distributed. I feel warranted only to make one observation and to give a brief description of the admittedly idiosyncratic approach that I take. The observation is that some faculty love to hate whatever salary system they are subjected to. Like many other people, they feel that they should be earning more, so the system must be at fault. But when approached about actually changing the system they love to hate, these same faculty are not always confident that things would be better in a new system. The point is simply that occasional grumbling about income seems to be a well-ingrained practice among faculty, not necessarily related to the level of their salaries or the fairness of a particular salary compensation program.

My approach is to devote at least half of the annual salary increase pool to across-the-board increases for all faculty (except those few who have clearly failed to contribute in any meaningful way to the common cause), not as a "cost-of-living" increase, but as a form of merit pay. That is, I believe that since the vast majority of "my" faculty do a fairly good job, they should all receive an increase on this account; those who haven't done a good job in any recognizable way should receive no increase at all. With the other half of the pool, then, merit "over and above" the

norm can be rewarded. Again, I tend to give at least some of this extra merit pay to virtually every faculty member, but some get a good deal more than others. Another feature of this system is that it gives faculty with higher salaries more money from the across-the-board increases (which are given in percentages), thus providing recognition for years of service and good performance (since those who have served longer and better tend to have the higher salaries). But the over-and-above merit increases are given in set-dollar amounts rather than percentages, so that the 30-year tenured faculty member judged to be at the top level of merit receives the exact same additional merit dollars as the first-year untenured faculty member who earned the same rating. This approach results, over all, in senior faculty receiving more actual dollars, but junior faculty receiving a higher percentage increase. What this means is that, over time, although the salaries of the good senior faculty continue to rise slowly from the pack, the entire pack tends to rise in concert, thus avoiding the creation of a radically salary-divided faculty. This works well in terms of overall equity and satisfaction, with exceptions representing the principle enunciated above, namely, that some people will never like the system to which they are subjected.

One final comment. Like most other deans, you will want to foster a genuine sense of academic community, a real cohesion among colleagues working together for common purposes. Differential salary increases can serve as wedges rather than as rewards. However, I have found that an open, public discussion of whether or not the community believes it is fair to recognize those who teach better, do better scholarly work, and contribute more to the governance of the institution, especially when many of these individuals clearly work harder and longer than those who do not perform as well as they do, leads easily to the conclusion that there should be some form of recognition of merit in the annual salary increase process. However, I am certain that part of the reason this works fairly well at my own institution is that our faculty salaries are good and the annual increase pool is always large enough to allow a reasonable increase even for those whose performance has been good but not exceptional.

My recommendation, then, is that all faculty should have good salaries and all deans should get a large annual salary increase pool! But whatever you do with the pool you actually receive, it is safe to assume that it will be appreciated more if your faculty think that your decisions are fair, based on impartial evidence, and consonant with publicly stated institutional values.

Evaluating Department Chairs

Elizabeth Scarborough, Indiana University, South Bend

The dean's evaluation of department chairs is an ongoing challenge—and opportunity—that includes both informal and formal elements. The process is a challenge because performance evaluation of close colleagues is a task that requires great sensitivity. Few persons, especially those new to the job, seem to undertake it with great enthusiasm or confidence. Nevertheless, carefully crafted and conducted systematic evaluations provide the opportunity to shape a faculty member's behavior by identifying conduct that deserves praise or requires change. Perhaps your greatest challenge is to create a cultural context in which both parties—evaluators and evaluated—view evaluation not merely as an institutional requirement but as a regularized opportunity for assessing progress toward achieving mutual goals.

Informally, you "evaluate" chairs quite regularly, by making judgments about how they are doing and providing them with informal feedback, guidance, and com-

mendation. Chair A develops a pattern of always coming in just after the announced deadline for providing a report, every report; Chair B writes faculty evaluations that are exorbitantly flattering for all, while confiding that the assistant professor on tenure probationary status really isn't doing very well in the classroom, but "I don't want to discourage him with a negative review"; Chair C devises a clever and original way of distributing faculty workload so that the schedule of the department is not negatively affected when one member needs extra time for a special research project; Chair D passes on to the dean an unusually large number of unresolved student complaints concerning the grading practices of a senior professor. Week by week, if not day by day, you are provided examples of the work performance of department chairs and thereby you compile, perhaps without awareness, an "implicit" evaluation of each.

"Evaluation," however, usually refers to a formal process that may take the form of an annual report followed by an annual evaluation, which may serve as the basis for merit pay increases, or a more extensive evaluation conducted as the basis for a reappointment decision. My present institution requires annual reports (i.e., evaluations) for each faculty member up to the level of the chief academic officer. Upon encountering this system and the great variety presented to me in the first round of reports, I found it helpful to provide some direction for the preparation of the "administrative" portion of the chairs' reports, asking them to organize their reports under five headings: Program Management, Personnel Management, Fiscal Management, Planning and Development, and Affirmative Action. [The first four topics thanks to Allan Tucker and Robert Bryan in *The Academic Dean: Dove, Dragon, and Diplomat*, (ACE, 1988); recommended!—see Section II-D of this Handbook]. This helped focus our attention upon the major tasks under review, despite the repugnance with which academics regard that alien term "management."

A danger with annual evaluations conducted in such a set format (for faculty as well as chairs) is that they may become hollow exercises: everyone gets a hearty pat on the back (and let's keep our fingers crossed for the next year!). Another danger is that both dean and chair may wait until the time of annual evaluation to deal with issues that should be addressed in a more timely way, on the "informal" schedule mentioned above. Taking the annual evaluation seriously as a vehicle for assessing the department and the chair's leadership and creating a climate in which difficulties can be identified and dealt with

as they arise are necessary to make good use of the annual evaluation. A matter of importance concerns how your evaluation is conveyed to the chair, whether in a face-to-face meeting or by written means. My preference is for an appointment followed by the written report, which becomes a matter of record in the personnel file. That may be less comfortable than the impersonal memo, but it does permit an interchange that may lead to focused problem solving.

Evaluation at the time of consideration for reappointment as chair is likely to involve department faculty in the formal process. Whether the chair is elected or appointed, the reappointment decision requires colleague input. You might use standardized, computer-scored, and normed evaluation instruments. Or you might rely on a report forwarded by the department as a whole after group discussion. Alternatively, you might call for individual faculty responses to be sent in writing or discussed in person, using either focused questions or an open-ended format. Having had experience with all of these, I would say the efficacy of each depends on the institution and departmental expectations. The value of faculty consultation depends on three essential elements. Faculty must be assured that their individual judgments will be held in confidence, even when you share with the chair the results of the process. They must believe that you are indeed open to hearing from the faculty rather than bringing to the process your own prejudgement of the outcome. And they must be confident that information provided will be taken seriously and used constructively.

Constructive use of evaluation results requires that clear expectations precede the evaluation itself and that the focus of the evaluation remains on tasks that have been identified and understood by both you and the chair. Regular joint goal-setting is one way of accomplishing this. Open communication—the courage and willingness to face up to problems as they occur—is also important. There should be no big surprises, positive or negative, at the time of the evaluation's delivery. Rather the evaluation conference should be a time of formal acknowledgment and planning for what needs to be accomplished in the future.

I find it wryly amusing, even as I shake my head, when I read occasionally in the advice literature: "If…, then you must replace the chair immediately." Due to department size and composition, the varying abilities and motivations faculty bring to their work, governance policy and practice, and other factors (you fill in *your* constraints!), the simple removal and replacement of an ineffective chair just is not possible for many of us. Rather, we must work patiently and skillfully, each within our own culture, knowing that much of our own effectiveness depends on that of the department chairs. Careful attention to the evaluation process can facilitate our efforts.

Retirement Arrangements for Faculty

Elizabeth Scarborough, Indiana University, South Bend

Given the demographics of the professorate, you should anticipate a record number of faculty retirements in the next decade. This despite the fact that professors appear to be setting a contrarian trend and choosing later rather than earlier retirement dates. "In 1993, only 84% of TIAA/CREF's participants had started to collect annuity income by age 70" (Robert K. Otterbourg, *Retire and Thrive*, New York: Kiplinger Books, 1995, p.17). For many faculty, retirement opens up opportunities to spend more time doing just what they love to do: reading, writing, traveling, thinking. For others, however, retirement threatens the loss of cherished experiences (e.g. interacting with students and colleagues), of resources for doing their research (lab facilities and subject pools), of the familiar routine of a regular schedule (meeting classes and attending faculty meetings). For the former, retirement is anticipated with eagerness; for the latter, dread and denial may dominate. For some,

retirement signifies "emancipation from the department"; for others, a loss of status or even selfhood. For all, retirement is a major life event, with implications that span economic, psychological, social, medical—and yes, existential—concerns.

What roles should you as dean play in this drama? Provide information, encourage planning and a realistic assessment of one's situation, ease the transition, honor past contributions and maintain commitment, press the issue a bit where necessary: these are some of the actions a dean might consider.

When I realized that many of our faculty—even those most active in faculty affairs—did not understand the very generous retirement benefits that our university provides at age 64, much less that Social Security requirements may be very important for them, I began the practice of sending out an explanatory letter each spring, to all aged 60 and above. This letter gives information on how to check on their benefits with the university and Social Security Administration as well as the requirements and procedures necessary to activate our plan. I note that the retirement plan can be activated very quickly once one meets certain requirements, but that departmental planning for replacement is greatly aided if we have lead time! At another institution, the Human Resources Office offered a series of six weekly two-hour sessions, open to faculty aged 60+, who were invited to attend with their spouses. Sessions focused on financial, health, occupational, recreational, residential, and relational considerations—a rundown on "what to expect and how to prepare and handle it." Each of these practices elicits both appreciative comments and, more importantly, conversations about retirement and its timing.

Whereas some faculty need the security blanket of a continuing institutional affiliation (though often for a shorter period of time than they think!), others maintain reciprocal and facilitating associations, and some take to the road quickly and happily sever all ties. Institutions differ, of course, on what services they can continue to provide retirees. At my university retirees receive reduced parking fee, use of library facilities, a computer account that provides access to the Internet, full membership in the Academic Senate and eligibility to serve on committees, invitations to participate in all official university functions (with academic garb provided if needed), and free or reduced admission to fee-bearing events. The departments determine whether to provide lab facilities, office space, clerical services, and copying privileges to retired faculty. In addition, retired faculty are invited once a year to a luncheon hosted by the chancellor.

Another institution (from which I took early retirement at age 56 before coming to my present job) supports a very active organization for retired faculty and professional staff, with quarterly get-togethers, a regular newsletter, and occasional service activities that support both the college and the community. Retired faculty can represent a valuable asset for various institutional functions; providing for their continued contacts with the institution and each other is one way of honoring their past service and valuable contributions.

One of the most difficult tasks for the administrator is to help a reluctant faculty member recognize when it is "time to go"—and to do so without incurring liability for age discrimination. Here's where your "people skills" really come into play! Mary Richards's short article has suggestions for that ("Counseling Faculty Member about Retirement" in *The Department Chair*, Spring 1992, pp.1 and 15). A summary of her key points: 1) inform yourself about the types of incentives the institution may offer; 2) use regular faculty development reviews; 3) learn the extracurricular interests of faculty; 4) identify what would be an attractive retirement package for a given person; 5) choose a neutral person to do the negotiations; and 6) be positive. In my recent experience, one faculty member needed accurate information and reassurance about his benefits. Another endured three years of unsatisfactory annual evaluations and no salary raises before making his decision. Yet another case involved gently confronting a 69-year-old with statements from mature and knowledgeable students that strongly suggested he was experiencing mini-seizures in class and really could not continue to meet his responsibilities.

Certainly it is important to inform yourself about the issues related to retirement decisions. A stumbling block for one of my faculty was that he had heard about the raising of the "full retirement" age for Social Security and thought he had to delay because of that. But he was born in 1931 and was relieved to learn that the new rules apply only to those born 1939 and later. Clay Schoenfeld's primer, *Retirement 901: A Comprehensive Seminar for Senior Faculty and Staff* (Magna, 1993), may help. It is poorly produced and would have benefited from some copy editing, but it touches on key points and has helpful information and useful references.

Schoenfeld (p. 52) cites an article by Donald Dudley, medical director of the Washington Institute of Neurosciences, Seattle ("Coping with retirement: Stress and life change" in *Journal of the College and University Personnel Association*, Summer 1991, pp.1-4), in which Dudley states: "The transition from being a worker to being a retiree is one of the most difficult and major life changes most of us will ever face.... People become increasingly stressed as they try to adapt to a new situation." With that in mind, good luck to us all!

FACULTY DEVELOPMENT

David E. Leary, University of Richmond

The quality of a college or university is determined, most crucially, by the quality of its faculty. Hence, there is no more important duty for you to perform as a dean than to assure the best possible hiring, mentoring, supporting, tenuring, and promoting of faculty. In brief, nothing is more important for the success of your institution—and thus for your own success—than faculty development. Whatever else you may be obliged to do, you should be most accountable for facilitating the teaching, research, and service efforts of your faculty. It is the faculty who teach, the faculty who do research, the faculty who engage in other kinds of creative and collegial activity. If you can help them teach better, accomplish more meaningful research, and participate more effectively—and even more enjoyably—in the local academic community, you will have done well.

In order to facilitate faculty development, you should do at least three things:

❖ Help establish clear expectations for faculty,

❖ Provide support and encouragement for faculty, and

❖ Implement appropriate forms of recognition and reward for faculty.

For many reasons, it is important that there be clear expectations for faculty performance, and that these be articulated in a collegial manner (with faculty participation) in light of the strategic mission, objectives, and initiatives of the faculty's department, school, and institution. (It is also important that these same expectations be kept in mind in the faculty hiring process: there is no use hiring one sort of person and then spending all your time trying to "develop" him or her into *another* kind of person.) Once expectations are clear, you should do whatever you can to provide appropriate support and encouragement. Although these will sometimes take the form of explicit recognitions and rewards (e.g., teaching awards and salary increases), they can and should also take many other forms, as illustrated below. The basic point, however, is that support, encouragement, recognition, and rewards should all be given in relation to the mission, objectives, and initiatives of the faculty members' departments, school, and institution. Sending mixed messages about what is salient to professional and institutional development can only detract from the achievement of an academic community's goals.

Faculty development is too often conceived as faculty remediation. No one can deny that there are times when you will need to deal with faculty whose performance has fallen below a reasonable standard. It is important, in such instances, to have both manner and means for prompting better performance, ideally through encouragement and support but if necessary through command and threat. My own experience suggests that it is best to avoid having a faculty member feel embarrassed or threatened, if this is at all possible.

With first offenses and complaints, unless they are of an egregious nature, I have found it useful to send a memo to the faculty member, with a copy to his/her chair, saying "I have heard that…. I have no idea if this is true or not, and I have no desire to have a response from you about this. I assume you will have a different perspective on this matter. I just want you to know the perception has been passed along to me, and I ask you to discuss it with your chairperson. If I hear nothing along this line again, you will hear nothing further from me and there will be no other reflection of this communication." This has often brought about the desired change, without creating a defensiveness or subsequent awkwardness on the part of the faculty member. In some cases, you must be prepared to go further, but the characteristics of further action are generally particular to the individual case, so there isn't much to say about them, except that you should be both as objective and as sensitive as possible in dealing with such matters.

The more typical case for faculty development involves faculty who are already good, or at least adequate, in their performance. The objective is not remediation but improvement, for the sake of the individual, the institution, and its students. Faculty improvement schemes within this context should be proactive rather than reactive, and they should be seen by faculty as being supportive rather than manipulative. In short, they should represent something offered *for* faculty rather than something done *to* them.

Having established this basic principle, there is no limit to the number of creative and useful programs that you can support. The goal of such programs is "creating a culture of growth and development" among the faculty, a culture which can and will rub off on students. Faculty too need to learn; faculty too need to do independent research; faculty too need to contribute to the welfare of their local community—this should be the message that students get, explicitly and implicitly, from faculty development programs. Indeed, some of these programs might be extended to students themselves.

Some of the faculty-development programs sponsored at my institution are:
❖ a year-long orientation program for new faculty;

- ❖ a variety of voluntary faculty reading groups;
- ❖ a faculty seminar for those preparing to teach in a common core course;
- ❖ a faculty seminar abroad;
- ❖ a lunchtime forum series for the sharing of ongoing research;
- ❖ a faculty newsletter;
- ❖ a faculty electronic-exchange network;
- ❖ a proactive annual review system, including a special pretenure evaluation program;
- ❖ a series of teaching-related workshops and luncheon discussions, which supplement the other programs and resources offered through the University's Teaching Center;
- ❖ a voluntary program of classroom visitation and discussion of teaching;
- ❖ a generous program of support for teaching innovations, research, and professional travel.

None of these programs is very astonishing or unusual. All of them—and more—are going on at other institutions. The point is for you to design and implement such activities within the context of an overall faculty development strategy, and for the faculty to see the various programs as part of a total web of opportunities for faculty to get to know one another better, to share teaching and research interests, and to stimulate and challenge each other.

(Just by knowing one another better, whether through faculty parties or a faculty picture book, faculty are much more likely to establish meaningful connections and productive collaborations, all on their own.) Properly conceptualized and organized, even committee work can serve a faculty development purpose, especially if it is distributed broadly and fairly enough to protect individuals from undue burdens and distractions. Committees to develop new curricula or to address pressing problems are particularly good vehicles for faculty development, if faculty are given the right sorts of roles and responsibilities. Travel to visit other institutions where good things are happening, or to attend relevant conferences, can also be helpful in this context. Every proactive dean will have stories about faculty who have been spurred to greater achievement by getting involved in some important institutional initiative.

There is no need to elaborate additional specific examples. You will have to design and support programs that take into account your own institution's mission, objectives, an initiatives, not to mention its relative strengths and weaknesses. The point is simply that faculty development is the name of the game for any dean who wishes to build a better educational institution.

Faculty Loads, Special Compensation

Philip Glotzbach, University of Redlands

Every college or university needs a fair and consistent policy for assigning faculty work load, and that policy should be clearly stated in the institution's faculty handbook or faculty personnel manual. This policy should be sufficiently flexible to accommodate variations in faculty work from discipline to discipline, at different moments in a faculty member's career, and in response to different institutional needs. It also should enable you as dean to make principled exceptions to standard practice in response to unique situations. Beware of crafting a policy that is so formula-driven or rigid that it complicates or even precludes the administrative decision-making that often is needed to handle special cases.

DEFINING THE STANDARD FACULTY WORK LOAD

For obvious reasons, most discussions of faculty load begin with teaching, and your handbook should indicate clearly how a standard teaching load is configured at your institution. Your policy needs to take into account your faculty/student ratio, curricular-based staffing needs, the percentage of courses your institution will cover with adjunct faculty, your academic calendar, types of courses (e.g., are courses the same size such as 4 credits, or is there considerable variation?), and differences in kinds of teaching (e.g., laboratory sessions versus lecture classes) across departments. A teaching load can be specified in terms of courses or credit hours. For example, your policy could take these considerations into account by specifying a standard teaching load as six courses per year, distributed across two semesters and a January inter-session, or by defining it as 24 semester units per academic year.

Your work-load policy needs to accommodate both standard and nonstandard forms of teaching: not only large and small classes but also private music lessons, supervision of students in clinical settings, directing a major play or opera, and supervision of science labs. If your institution allows large classes (and even "large" will be a relative term), your policy needs to indicate at what point (if any) a faculty member will receive the help of a teaching assistant or grader and whether a class over a certain size might count in place of two smaller ones. Alternatively, can faculty at your institution fulfill their teaching obligations by offering only small courses, or do you also require them to serve a minimum number of students per quarter, semester, or academic year? For purposes of determining load, are co-taught courses counted the same as regular courses, or is the teaching "credit" per faculty member reduced?

The complexity of such questions makes it difficult, if not impossible, to set any simple policy (or formula) for achieving equity of faculty load across an entire institution. For example, if you require a certain number of courses (or course equivalents), some faculty will necessarily teach more students per unit of time than others (e.g., creative writing faculty offering intensive writing workshops, which should be no larger than 15, will usually teach fewer students per semester or quarter than faculty in psychology whose load includes some larger introductory sections). Some courses carry heavier expectations for grading papers, as contrasted with courses that emphasize exams. So you need to approach these issues with a judicious sense of faculty work that starts with reasonable disciplinary expectations. Broader curricular needs play an important role as well. For example, a physics department in a small liberal arts college will typically serve a much smaller number of majors than will a comparably-sized sociology or philosophy department. But small upper-division courses for physics majors can be balanced by expecting the department to make a vigorous contribution to the general education curriculum through lower-division courses for nonscience majors, first-year seminars, etc.

As a rule of thumb, you should be involved primarily in working with the appropriate faculty committee(s) to establish the most general level of policy. Next you should work with your department chairs to ensure that as much as possible the more detailed work of configuring individual faculty teaching loads occurs within the department (with the high bid being that this is a collaborative process in which all department members participate). It will probably be necessary to approve some special arrangements that various departments need to make to accommodate their individual situations (e.g., to agree to an equivalency between a set amount of clinical supervision or a set number of hours of private music lessons and a course). Once approved, such arrangements should be administered departmentally. You definitely do not want to be in the business of personally negotiating all faculty loads each quarter or semester. Even so, you or your associate dean should review (or spot-check) faculty teaching loads regularly, a part of the normal review of the course schedules proposed by individual departments. Well-run departments with effective, well-trained department chairs will make this review a simple matter; obviously, more troubled departments or departments with less effective chairs will require closer attention from your office.

Make sure that you go over the general faculty load policy as well as your expectations for particular departments with new department chairs at the time of their appointment.

Beyond teaching assignments narrowly conceived, an institution's faculty work-load policy should clarify the additional expectations that apply. You might not want to stipulate a minimum number of office hours per week, but you probably do want to state the expectation that faculty set and keep office hours (and also make themselves available to students by appointment). Every college or university has an expectation for continuing faculty development—research or creative activity—and that should be described. Finally, you need to be clear about your expectations for service. There is general work in every department, academic program, college, and university, and faculty need to contribute their fair share. Individual faculty members will do this in different ways, according to their abilities and interests, and accordingly this part of the faculty work load should be described in as flexible a way as possible. Moreover, faculty will take on different load profiles at different times depending upon their focus in a given year (e.g., developing a new course, starting up or completing a research project, or assuming a particularly heavy service load), and your load policy needs to acknowledge and indeed, encourage such healthy variation.

NORMAL VARIATIONS

Your institution's policy regarding a standard teaching load should accommodate such normal and recurring work as independent studies, overseeing senior projects and honors theses, directing student research in science, and so on. Many of these tasks are best regarded as a regular part of a full-time teaching faculty load (e.g., offering a reasonable number of independent studies, sitting on a reasonable number of honors committees). However, "excessive" responsibilities should be factored into load (e.g., the assignment of overseeing all the senior projects of a substantial-sized program in a given year might automatically count as a course). Once again, how these matters are handled will vary by institution. But there should be a sense across departments in a given college or university that, in general, teaching load is distributed equitably.

ACCOMMODATING EXCEPTIONS

No matter how well your general policy for allocating faculty load is conceived and administered, from time to time the dean or associate dean will be called upon to sanction exceptions and adjudicate difficult or complex cases. You need to bring to such negotiations a clear understanding of your general policy, a well-articulated set of principles that guide you in making exceptions, and your own sense of fairness. Never conclude an individual negotiation without checking with the appropriate department chair or before satisfying yourself that the accommodation you are contemplating in one case is consistent with decisions you have made (or would want to make in the future) in other similar situations. It is always good to take a request under advisement and render a final decision on a later occasion, after having consulted appropriately and given full consideration to the broader implications of that individual case.

Both faculty and administrators sometimes think first of the two obvious ways to accommodate exceptions to the normal load that involve extraordinary work (e.g., chairing a particularly demanding governance committee, trying to complete a research project in a given semester): released time from teaching or overload pay. I discuss these options below, but I would urge you to consider a third alternative before resorting to the two most obvious ones. This third option is to begin with a comprehensive view of a standard load—teaching, research/creative activity, and service—and look first for trade-offs in the non-teaching portion. For example, a faculty member who needs to complete a book manuscript to meet a publisher's deadline might be released from normal (departmental and institutional) service expectations for a quarter or semester or even for a year. Assuming that service is a serious expectation for all faculty (and it should be), release from service expectations can be just as significant as release from a course. Likewise, a faculty member who assumes a burdensome administrative task (e.g., chairing a contentious department) can be released from research expectations for a limited period of time, with such a release noted by the dean in an official memo to file that will be included in the faculty member's next review. Obviously such an option may not be appropriate for a faculty member whose next review deals with tenure or promotion, but in other cases it can work. Often it is the best teachers who are called upon to perform other special tasks. Removing them from the classroom may not be as

attractive an institutional option as the alternatives noted here. Furthermore, it is not in any institution's best interest to create a climate of expectation—or worse, a sense of entitlement—that faculty will be regularly released from teaching obligations to perform necessary faculty work.

Nevertheless, there are times when the preceding options will not work and you have to consider granting release from teaching. Your general work-load policy should outline a set of basic options. It is better to write that policy as a description of practice than to establish hard and fast rules. So you should look first at current practice and determine whether it is reasonably consistent (e.g., every chair of a department above a certain minimum size receives one course release per year) or whether current practice is a structure of special deals that have been cut at different times, with different departments or faculty, and perhaps even by different administrators. One heuristic you can use in examining current practice is to ask how comfortable you would be in defending it publicly, in detail. Could you articulate the principles that warranted a course release in one case but not in another? If not, then you have some conceptual work to do. If you have good principles, then write them down, both for your own use and as a help to your successor.

Sometimes a course release just is not an option (e.g., if the problem is that a department needs an extra course and it is not possible to bring in someone from outside to teach it), and in such cases you may need to consider additional compensation. Occasionally, it is possible to trade present service for future concessions (e.g., if you teach the extra course this semester, I'll give you a course release next fall). On other occasions it will be necessary to provide additional salary or a stipend. Once again, it is important to have a policy that is fair, as consistent as possible, and that makes distinctions that can be justified by principle.

Most schools have a standard per-course rate of compensation for adjunct faculty. That rate should be used as well to set compensation for full-time faculty for teaching an additional course. Such a practice is preferable—and far cheaper to the institution—to offering someone a percentage of her or his annual salary. You certainly do not want to establish a system that gives people an incentive to teach overloads. So make the compensation fair but not extravagant. If you believe you need to offer monetary compensation for other kinds of extraordinary work (e.g., taking on a second major committee assignment or a substantial administrative project that cannot be postponed), then try to equate the effort involved with that required to teach an "average" course. Is the extra assignment approximately equivalent to one-half or the full amount of the work required to teach a course? If

you can answer this question (even if only to your own satisfaction), then once again you can relate the compensation to your adjunct faculty scale. The point is to place such questions in relation to other practices to avoid as much as possible having to make ad hoc, arbitrary judgments.

CONCLUSION

The overall goal in developing and administering a faculty work-load policy is to help your faculty distribute their responsibilities in ways that not only are equitable but also are perceived to be equitable. So you need a consistent policy, and you should be able to break your own rules (occasionally) in the service of fairness. Just be sure that you can articulate to others, if challenged, the principles on which your exceptions are based. In the end, the highest praise faculty can give your policy is their indifference— regarding the rules as obvious, taking for granted that you will apply them in a fair and evenhanded manner, and assuming that any exception you make must be grounded in a good reason.

Incentive Programs

Peter A. Facione, Santa Clara University

ndividual faculty and academic departments have plenty to do. Often their goals, either as individuals concerned with their teaching and scholarship, or as departments concerned with their major programs and internal issues, do not permit the projects, programs, and priorities of the dean's office to percolate to the top of the list. While threats of lost resources and appeals to high principles may be part of the complex set of motivators you might consider using, and while you may even suggest that the individual's and the department's best long-term interests are served if they would give greater time and effort to a given project, these strategies often are insufficient, at least in themselves. But, on occasion, the judicious use of positive incentives can lubricate the wheels of institutional loyalty and reorient the focus of individuals and of departments toward those priorities and projects that are less focused on their individual interests and goals and more focused on the needs of the college or the university.

◆ INDIVIDUAL INCENTIVES

Perhaps the most important commodity to busy faculty is time. Thus release from teaching responsibilities is often what they seek. Sometimes faculty receive course releases to compensate for administrative services as program directors or chairs. Often faculty ask for a course release to work on an onerous task force, to complete a worthy and urgent creative or scholarly project, or to engage in time-consuming curricular, advising, or accreditation, or assessment projects. These options appear at least superficially attractive to the budget conscious dean, for the cost appears to be limited to the salary of the replacement instructor, if any. Usually in dollars this is a disproportionately small fraction of the cost of the full-time faculty member who is released. There are, however, other potential costs to be considered. Where the practice of using course releases flourishes, one finds significant numbers of sections in the general education program and, at times in the undergraduate major as well, taught by transient junior faculty whose institutional commitment and expertise often do not match that of the faculty member who was released. This can lead to serious problems with student academic advising, student retention, program integrity, and a host of personnel issues relating to the recruitment, training, supervision, and evaluation of temporary faculty.

Nationally, the percentage of sections taught by part-time and temporary faculty has increased steadily over several years, what with budget reductions, an increase in the significance of publication as a necessary condition for tenure and promotion, and the practice of motivating the best faculty to work on college and university projects through using course releases. Seeing this, some deans have begun to offer stipends or paid overloads instead of course releases. Often the dollar cost of the stipend equals, or may even exceed, the lowest level replacement cost paid to hire a part-time adjunct faculty member. But, in view of the other costs, the stipend may turn out in some cases to be a better deal for the college and the university. Then too, there are situations where a full course release is not warranted, but some modest incentive would be useful. Since stipends can come in very different sizes, it is easier for you to relate the size of the stipend to market conditions in order to motivate the person you want to take the job. Some deans use stipends in combination with course releases when the work is both time consuming and not directly related to the faculty member's own teaching and scholarship. Often department chairs receive some combination of both stipend and course release, for example.

Incentives to part-time faculty are often neglected, but can be quite useful tools. Most of us associate salary with teaching load for part-time faculty. The pay per course program at most institutions is quite simple: one course and the pay is X, two courses and the pay is twice X. Some institutions offer slightly higher pay to people based on their years of service or on the equivalent academic rank if they were full time. This variation is often found in summer programs and in continuing education, where even the college's regular full time faculty are eligible to earn extra pay. An interesting and useful variation on this is found in some summer programs where faculty are also offered higher salaries depending on course enrollments. Under this incentive program, those who offer to teach more popular courses, usually those courses that are needed to fulfill general education or major requirements in large enrollment areas, are issued contracts with a sliding scale based on enrollment as of a certain date.

The extent of a person's part-time contract has an impact on what fringe benefits are available. For example, at half-time work a contract written for six months or longer may trigger a health benefits package. Maybe at 75% time a tuition remission program, if there is one, becomes an added benefit. Perhaps at some other point a retirement program or a life insurance program becomes part of the mix. Different institutions have different policies in this regard. Some benefits, such as housing assistance, might be restricted only to tenured or tenure track faculty. Some benefits are mandated by state and federal employment rules. It is essential for responsible budgeting that you should learn the percentage of benefits costs associated with the time base and length of service for which contracts are issued.

At times you or the fiscal officer might think only of the financial bottom line, believing that by saving a few percentage points of benefits costs the institution is coming out ahead. But from both an ethical and a professional perspective it is wise to be mindful that persons who accept temporary contracts are highly educated people who can usually be counted on to be quite responsible in the execution of their teaching duties. Many of us started in this profession in exactly that way, as temporary and part-time adjunct instructors. This is not a reason to continue or to expand exploitation, but an invitation to remember the troubles of our early careers and eliminate the abuse of part-time adjunct faculty. One clear way is to offer higher pay per course. But it may be better to offer contracts that run for the whole academic year and which include enough teaching to trigger access to key institutional benefits programs, such as health insurance. Health insurance coverage can also be very useful as an incentive to persons, even if the per-course salary is not as high as paid by the college down the road. The loyalty purchased by such a program can often be more valuable to the students and the college than the relatively small dollar cost of adding more faculty to the health benefits group policy.

Another incentive option is to use some of the more talented part-time academic year faculty to do those very projects for which one was trying earlier to motivate full-time tenured and tenure-track faculty. Here an

added stipend to a part-time faculty member to undertake an assessment project, to serve as an academic advisor, to run the learning lab, to oversee the student media, etc. can be a mutually beneficial strategy.

The concept of incentives to individual faculty, particularly the sliding contract idea, can be extended. For example, as a response to the call for more full-time faculty to teach in the freshman and sophomore general education program, you might browbeat department chairs to change the teaching schedules of long-time tenured faculty. This might achieve a small victory in a department or two, but the prospects of massive change in the face of long-standing departmental cultures that relegate teaching "service courses" to the bottom of the prestige pile is unlikely. An alternative is to use positive incentives. You might, for example, offer sliding contracts to new full-time persons not on the tenure track. The offer of hire might indicate that for a given salary the person will teach X courses, but for a higher salary X+1 courses, and for a still higher salary X+2 courses. This is, in effect, to offer a paid overload option at point of hire. With continuing faculty this option can be introduced as well. One might, for example, offer to increase the base pay of continuing faculty for their agreement to a permanent change in their teaching responsibilities which would then increase by some proportionate number of courses. Again, this can be seen as an agreement to a permanent paid overload or as an agreement to amend the terms and conditions of employment for an identifiable sub-group of faculty through the processes of individual negotiation or collective negotiation.

DEPARTMENTAL INCENTIVES

Nothing works better than more money, except perhaps more positions and more space. But you usually will not be provided with the resources to quench the thirst of even one department, to say nothing of the eager and persistent demands of many departments. A great deal of good will, more careful understanding, and mutual support can be achieved by a full and honest sharing of budget and resource information, and by the development of fair and open procedures or protocols for the internal allocation and use of resources within the college. Yet, without some carrots, what are you to do in the face of apathy and indifference to institutional mandates and the needs of the college as a whole? One option is to create incentive programs internal to the college, if not the university, to motivate departments in a positive way.

Return Year-End Budget Surplus. One of the most frustrating things about fiscal year budgeting is that at the end of the fiscal year a department loses what it does not spend. Beside the flurry of purchase orders this generates, the department is being rewarded for exactly the wrong behavior. In fact, shortsighted administrators have often thought that underspending was a sign of overly generous allocations! The more cynical chairs, particularly those who feel that the college owes them a larger budget anyway, will think little of overspending, perhaps knowing that the dean will have to cover the difference. This pattern can be turned around quickly by the practice of carrying forward budget surpluses and budget deficits from one fiscal year to the next. Yes, most budgets have rules against this.

Often called the "current unrestricted fund" or "fiscal year budget," accounting procedures as well as good management practices, call for first and second level units to return unused money at the end of the fiscal year. To implement a program of 100% returns, the administrator at the next level up must keep separate track of end-of-year budget shortfalls and budget surpluses. Then, at the start of the new fiscal year, out of a different fund which does carry from year to year—and there are many, such as discretionary accounts, gift accounts, capital project accounts, or overhead accounts—the budget administrator simply supplements those departments that ended the previous fiscal year in the black by the amount that they were in the black. An easy augmentation to this approach is reducing the new fiscal year's budget of those units that ended in the red. A useful variation is not to supplement or debit the operating budgets of departments but instead to create gift accounts for each department. This way you can reward those departments that end in the black by transferring, in the equivalent amount, from your own gift account to theirs. Obviously, before starting this program at your institutions, you should check very carefully with your fiscal officers to learn the rules of budgeting that apply to your situation—those that come from good accounting practice as well as those that might come from what the Board, president, or vice president will permit.

Tuition Revenue Sharing. To motivate participation in a program, such as the summer program or continuing education, you might craft a revenue sharing policy that returns some fraction of the gross (or net) tuition to the department. This is a useful way to motivate departments and department chairs to seek good courses and good instructors for these programs. It is also a useful way to recognize that there are costs to the departments and to the chairs for supporting these programs. The most obvious costs might be those associated with staff time and course supplies. But there can be other costs, such as the time spent to find good faculty to teach the courses that the summer program director might wish to have offered, or the time needed to address student complaints or advising needs arising from the summer or continuing education program. Revenue sharing from tuition paid, particularly if it goes beyond simply the trivial costs of supplies and direct expenses, can go a long way toward ameliorating these issues.

Revenue Sharing, Attractive Venues. Some departments are able to generate revenues, or not, given the availability of external funding in their disciplines or the special nature of their academic facilities. Theaters, museums, concert halls, and athletic fields and facilities, for example, can be valuable revenue generators during the summer months and during those relatively rare times in the academic year when not being used for student-related events and performances. Revenue is available from renting the facility as well as from ticket and concessions sales. All too often, however, there is no incentive to the academic department that controls the venue. Without something to show for their effort, departments are unwilling to put themselves through the trouble and expense associated with preparing contracts and securing the equipment that will make the venue suitable for larger

scale rental and revenue producing activities. At the same time, the same department often finds itself in need of expensive equipment upgrades and capital improvements. A program of revenue sharing that covers the added staffing costs and operating expenses and that provides additional funds to the department to upgrade equipment and make physical improvements can turn a negative situation into a very positive one. This is one example where less to the university's bottom line this year can end up being more for the department and the university in the long run.

Overhead from Grants and Fund Raising. Institutions usually have a well discussed, and hotly contested, policy on how grant overhead and fund-raising revenue is to be shared among the president's office and the vice presidents, and, at times, the deans. Frequently the percentage returned to the department—or to the individual investigator in the case of grant overhead—is too small to be a serious incentive. This, however, may not be the wisest policy from the point of view of building capacity in the long run. You might, for example, negotiate for 100% return of grant overhead to the college and then create a program internal to the college that gives incentives to the department and faculty members who received the grant, and perhaps also uses some of the remaining overhead to support other grant-writing activities in the department and college. A dean might negotiate for a percentage of fund-raising revenue, particularly when college faculty and students are used to staff telephone solicitation campaigns, as a way of supporting those departments that provide the faculty and students for those efforts. It is one thing for us to call on the good will of students and faculty occasionally, it is another to call on their good will and then offer in return some sharing of the fruits of that labor.

Departments often ask for the allocation of new faculty positions to support the development of their academic majors. Even with all the quantitative and qualitative data that we now have, it is difficult to decide which of several departments to reward with a tenure-track hiring opportunity. And even that does not guarantee that the broader needs of the general education program or faculty diversity will be met. However, a program of designating positions for support of particular academic goals can be a very positive inducement to departments. One example, crafted in support of the general education program, provides for departments to make proposals with regard to how, if

awarded a new tenure-track position, they would offer in return six more sections of general education courses taught by tenured or tenure-track faculty. Obviously, the new hire would not be expected to teach all, or maybe any, of those six sections. But the department, which would then have the faculty line to support adding six sections to its course offerings, would be expected to adjust teaching assignments of whomever it wished, provided that the net gain to the general education program was six more sections taught by tenured or tenure-track faculty. Once filled, that position remains with the department, along with the added responsibility for those six sections, until it is vacated. Then the position reverts back to the general education program and can become, once again, the subject for new proposals from the same and other departments.

5

Legal Matters

ACAD

AMERICAN CONFERENCE OF ACADEMIC DEANS

AFFIRMATIVE ACTION/EQUAL OPPORTUNITY

Bari Watkins, Morningside College

Affirmative action programs make special efforts to benefit persons in legally protected classes in order to compensate for past discrimination. Protected classes include race, color, national origin, religion, sex, age, and disability. Except by local ordinance, sexual orientation is not a protected category. In the past, affirmative action programs could be court ordered or adopted voluntarily. Equal opportunity regulations, by contrast, simply seek to prohibit discrimination against such persons.

In the mid-1990s, legal issues concerning affirmative action programs are undergoing the most dramatic changes seen in decades. Equal opportunity regulations are not engendering major criticism or modification.

The information presented here is meant to provide you with general guidance. Major institutional decisions focused on affirmative action should always be made with advice of counsel.

◆ AFFIRMATIVE ACTION

Voluntary affirmative action (AA) programs (in admissions and hiring) are heavily debated. Some believe that non-beneficiaries are disadvantaged by such programs; others argue that those intended as beneficiaries are stigmatized by affirmative action.

Until 1978, the Supreme Court supported college and university AA programs that met a compelling government interest, which was defined as addressing past local discrimination or attracting a diverse student body. In the famous 1978 decision, *Regents of the University of California v. Bakke*, the court found that numerical quotas were unconstitutional except in remediation of immediate past discrimination, but an institution could legitimately use race as a "plus factor," or "one element in a range of factors a university may properly consider" in an attempt to create diversity in the student body. Four justices were opposed to any approval of affirmative action programs; four others wanted to continue allowing the use of race to remedy the effects of past discrimination, even if there was no recent history of discrimination at the institution doing the remediating. Justice Lewis Powell alone, in an attempt to build a consensus, proposed the "plus factor" notion to create a narrow bridge between the two groups; none of his colleagues explicitly accepted this compromise. Thus the fragile construction of a sole justice had held together a legal balance until recent years. During that time, most colleges and universities carefully eschewed using an explicit racial quota and instead adopted the "plus factor" criterion in admissions and hiring decisions.

The Powell compromise began to unravel in 1995. In May, the Supreme Court refused to review a lower court ruling that invalidated a scholarship program limited to black students at the University of Maryland at College Park. The University asked for a review on the grounds that many other schools offered similar race-specific scholarships. By refusing to review, the Supreme Court left the decision legally binding in the Fourth Circuit (Maryland, North Carolina, South Carolina, Virginia, and West Virginia). Schools in those states should probably avoid advertising race-specific opportunities. The decision could also be cited as precedent in lawsuits elsewhere in the country, but it does not have the force of law. [Scott Jaschik, "'No' on Black Scholarships," *Chronicle of Higher Education*, June 2, 1995, p. A25].

In June of the same year, the Supreme Court ruled 5-4 that federal programs or polices based on race or ethnicity must meet a legal test of "strict scrutiny"

(*Adarand Constructors, Inc. v. Pena*). That means that the program would have to demonstrate a "compelling government interest" in its work and be "narrowly tailored" to meet its specific goals. This decision did not directly affect college or university programs, but it did cover a wide variety of programs run by federal agencies, some of which award grants to minority students and faculty members or set aside research dollars for traditionally black colleges. The Congressional Research Office identified about 40 such programs in a 1995 study. [Scott Jaschik, "Blow to Affirmative Action," *Chronicle of Higher Education*, June 23, 1995, pp. A21-A23].

The *Hopwood* decision of March, 1996 has drawn the most attention for dismantling affirmative action in college and university admissions. In this case, four white applicants sued the University of Texas School of Law because they were denied admission; they alleged violation of their rights under the equal protection clause of the 14th Amendment. The institution, which used an elaborate admissions system, did in fact treat blacks and Mexican Americans differently from other categories of applicants.

The U.S. District Court for the Fifth District found that the law school had violated equal protection, but refused to prohibit the law school from using race in admissions decisions. On March 29, 1996 the US Court of Appeals reversed the lower court decision, ruling that race could not be used to decide which applicants to admit. Under the "strict scrutiny" standard mandated by *Adarand*, the court found that consideration of race or ethnicity for the purpose of achieving a diverse student body was not a compelling justification for race-based discrimination in admissions. Thus the school of law, "is prohibited from considering race in any manner in its admissions process" [*Hopwood v. State of Texas.* 78 F3d 932].

The Supreme Court declined to review the *Hopwood* decision, therefore allowing it to stand as law in the fifth district: Texas, Louisiana, and Mississippi. Colleges and universities in those states should show great prudence concerning their existing policies and practices. ACAD deans should certainly confer with each other as well as with counsel on this important matter. Absent a Supreme Court review, *Hopwood* does not apply in other judicial districts, but the decision could well be used as a part of a lawsuit in other areas.

To date, California is the only state with legislation outlawing affirmative action programs. The California Civil Rights Initiative (CCRI, passed in November of 1996 as Proposition 209 and upheld in the courts on appeal) amends the state constitution to read: "The state shall not discriminate against, or grant preferential treatment to, any individual or group on the basis of race, sex, color, ethnicity, or national origin in the operation of public employment, public education, or public contracting." To date, major research universities in California, medical schools, and law schools report marked declines in minority enrollment.

In summary, the University of Maryland decision means that institutions in the fourth circuit (Maryland, North Carolina, South Carolina, Virginia, and West Virginia) may not offer scholarships directed solely at members of a racial or ethnic group. The decision may be used in the future in law suits in other areas. The *Hopwood* decision means that institutions in the fifth district (Texas, Louisiana, and Mississippi) may not consider race "in any manner" in admissions decisions. That decision, too, may be used in future lawsuits in other districts. The CCRI in California outlaws affirmative action programs in the state through a constitutional change. These difficult and rapidly changing circumstances demand caution from academic institutions.

EQUAL OPPORTUNITY GUIDELINES

There are two major goals for equal opportunity efforts: to avoid actual discrimination against persons in protected classes, and to avoid the appearance of such discrimination. A wise dean has commented that you don't want to be vulnerable to charges of making the right choice for the wrong reason—that is, to fail to appoint someone for sound reasons but leave yourself open to the charge of having made that decision on the basis of an impermissible factor like race, age, or gender.

By now, virtually every institution in the United States has developed guidelines and mandated practices to avoid discrimination and the appearance of discrimination. Some have created scripts for interviews, others videotape interviews or require interview witnesses. Most are less stringent. You should make sure that all procedures at your institution are reviewed regularly and followed carefully.

In addition, however, you need also to work with faculty on how to handle the less structured portions of interviews: dinners with search committees, rides from the airport, etc. It is in those settings that questionable behavior can most easily happen. Remind faculty that they may not inquire about a candidate's family, personal life, or similar matters until and unless the candidate introduces information voluntarily. Even then, it is not good to pursue such areas very extensively. Faculty should be reminded that we are all accustomed in ordinary life to pursue conversations with new acquaintances by inquiring about exactly the areas they should avoid in interviews. It takes a special effort, for example, not to use a question about children as an opening gambit in a social conversation.

Many people confuse equal opportunity regulations with AA programs and thus assume that recent court decisions about AA somehow affect protections against discrimination. It would be reasonable to assume that some will be less careful to avoid the appearance of discrimination given the changed judicial and political climate. You should therefore take on the responsibility of educating a college community about the distinction and about the continued importance of making personnel decisions fairly and in accordance with the law.

Dismissals, Non-Renewals, Terminations

H. Dale Abadie, Craft Institute for International Studies, University of Mississippi

Few decisions involving the dean are as painful and as costly to the institution as those involving the dismissal, non-renewal, or termination of faculty. They are accompanied by pain and discomfort because those decisions almost always reflect failure of some kind: failure on the part of the faculty member to meet or adjust to institutional expectations; failure of the institution to make sound judgments in the hiring process with regard to the faculty member's potential for serving the objectives of the college or university; or, perhaps, the failure of the school to contribute successfully to the faculty member's professional development.

The decision to sever the employment relationship can be costly on a number of levels. There is the cost of institutional resources expended in an unsuccessful attempt at faculty development. On occasion, there are the expenses associated with severance settlements and negotiated arrangements. And, perhaps most costly, is the effect of the separation upon the faculty member's professional advancement. For all of those reasons, there is often an institutional reluctance to embark upon dismissal, non-renewal, or termination proceedings. However, there are times when institutional well-being requires it.

Although often confused because closely related, the terms "dismissal" and "termination" have different meanings. Both usually apply to separation "for cause," dismissal referring to the ending of a faculty member's employment prior to the expiration of his or her term appointment, and termination applying to the ending of employment upon completion of the term of appointment. Both terms, and especially "termination," are used in cases involving tenured faculty, whereas "non-renewal" has to do with decisions not to renew the employment contract of a non-tenured faculty member.

A few words of caution should precede discussion of the processes for ending employment of faculty members. The suggestions that follow are not intended to apply where an institution is party to a collective bargaining agreement. In those cases, it is likely that your actions are limited by the terms and procedural requirements of the specific agreement. Also, you should be mindful of the fact that institutions vary considerably and that each has specific and differing procedures for dealing with such matters. Therefore, especially if you are a new dean or one new to your institution, you should become familiar with your school's standards and procedures pertaining to employment and personnel issues. For example, public universities often are regulated by procedures established by state governing boards and require the involvement of state offices, such as the Office of the Attorney General. Private colleges usually have procedures established or at least sanctioned by boards of trustees.

Although the courts have generally declined to become involved in the non-renewal of contracts of non-tenured faculty on the grounds that those individuals do not have a property right associated with employment, most colleges and universities subscribe to the procedural standards of the American Association of University Professors (AAUP). AAUP standards require that faculty who are not to be renewed receive timely, written notice: no later than March 1, or three months, for faculty in the first academic year of service; no later than December 15, or six months, for faculty in the second academic year of service; and at least 12 months before the expiration of an

appointment for those who have been in the institution for two or more years. Ordinarily the reasons for non-renewal decisions need not be given. Most institutions have separate procedures for dealing with the appeals of faculty who claim that the decision not to renew one's contract involves a violation of a constitutional (usually first amendment) right.

Because termination processes apply to tenured faculty, questions concerning them are examined with closer scrutiny by the academic and legal communities. This has proven to be the case in recent years where termination has occurred for reasons of "financial exigency." If your school is faced with conditions of financial exigency, you would do well to review carefully the AAUP standards relative to the use of financial exigency for terminations and, especially, to maintain close consultation with the institution's legal counsel and higher administrative officials. Such coordination and consultation are important in all considerations for dismissal or termination, but, because of the possibility of litigation, they take on a special urgency where financial exigency is the reason for this action.

Termination of faculty "for cause" is a less common occurrence and requires not only that the cause for the separation be sufficient and clearly established, but that separation occur only after due process has been accorded the faulty member concerned. Thus, the procedure used to accomplish the termination is an extremely important factor once a decision to terminate has been made. Though procedures vary among institutions, a few common principles apply to actions of this type:

❖ Institutions may relieve faculty of duties pending proceedings if there is substantial reason to believe that immediate harm is threatened by continuance of the faculty member in his or her duties.

❖ If termination or dismissal is being considered, the faculty member must be notified of this and offered the right to request a hearing.

❖ Faculty should be presented with a statement of charges and provided with sufficient time to prepare a defense.

❖ At a hearing, the faculty member should be permitted to be heard in his or her defense and to have present an advisor who may act as counsel.

❖ The faculty member should have the right to present witnesses as well as to question witnesses, and the right to a full stenographic record of the hearing without cost.

Those procedural safeguards are consistent with AAUP principles and have generally met the basic requirements of institutional due process required by the courts. That they might involve significant investments of time, attention, and monetary costs testifies at once to the seriousness of terminations and dismissals and to the hesitancy of institutions to invoke them where alternative actions are possible. Thus you should proceed with termination or dismissal proceedings only after consultation with the college or university legal counsel and after obtaining the concurrence of the institution's chief executive officer.

Legal Matters

HARASSMENT

Lisa A. Rossbacher, Southern Polytechnic State University

116

*Resource
Handbook
for
Academic
Deans*

Harassment can be broadly considered as a type of discrimination, on the basis of age, race, class, religion, ethnicity, economic back ground, gender, or other factors. Harassment may take many forms, but the most common ones that a dean encounters are likely to be related to sexual harassment.

The standard definition of sexual harassment was originally developed by the Equal Employment Opportunity Commission in 1980, in Guidelines on Discrimination Because of Sex:

> Unwelcome sexual advances, requests for sexual favors, and other verbal or physical conduct of a sexual nature...when (1) submission to such conduct is made either explicitly or implicitly a term or condition of an individual's employment, (2) submission to or rejection of such conduct by an individual is used as the basis for employment decisions affecting such individual, or (3) such conduct has the purpose or effect of substantially interfering with an individual's work performance by creating an intimidating, hostile, or offensive working environment.

The EEOC language was adopted in a Supreme Court decision in 1986, and it is still the standard definition of sexual harassment. Colleges and universities have significant responsibility (and therefore liability) in ensuring that the working environment is free of harassment for all employees. The following advice is directed toward minimizing both occurrences and liability for sexual harassment.

1. The best protection is for a college to have a clear statement of policy and procedures on sexual harassment.
   a. If a harassment policy already exists for your campus, take a careful look at it, and ask questions about how responsive it has proven to be in actual use. Be sure it ensures rapid resolution of problems when they arise. If a policy does not exist, develop one as quickly as possible, involving men and women faculty

and students, and consult carefully with your institution's legal counsel—but don't automatically do everything the lawyers say, unless it makes sense to you.

b. In addition to specifying what behavior is not acceptable, the harassment policy should include specific, relatively-easy-to-follow procedures for how to resolve complaints.

c. Both an informal and a formal process should be available, with only the formal part of the process resulting in sanctions.

d. Confidentiality should be maintained for everyone involved, as much as possible. Among the most difficult cases to resolve are those in which the accuser will not permit her or his name to be used (or to be otherwise identified to the alleged harasser).

e. The harassment policy should include a specific policy on romantic or sexual relationships between students and faculty.

f. The entire policy should be included in the faculty handbook or an equivalent document that makes adherence to the policy a condition of employment. A common way to address this is to place sexual harassment clearly under the category of unprofessional conduct that threatens the academic freedom of other members of the community.

2. All complaints, responses, and ultimate outcomes should be recorded; all the records should be kept in a single, confidential location.

3. Every complaint, whether formal or informal, should be investigated; this is often an important factor in later identification of institutional liability.

4. A single individual (or office) should receive all formal complaints. It can be helpful if several people (men and women) are identified as being available to help with informal resolution, but they must be consistent in their record-keeping. The involvement of the dean at this stage is a college-specific decision: some colleges identify the dean as the point person for cases involving faculty, while other colleges prefer to keep the dean out of the process in order to serve at the appeal level, if needed.

5. In conjunction with the harassment policy, colleges should also have a specific program to ensure that students, faculty, and staff are informed about their right to be free from sexual harassment.

Note: The information included here should not be used in place of qualified legal advice!

SUGGESTED REFERENCES

Fitzgerald, L., 1992. *Sexual Harassment in Higher Education: Concepts and Issues.* National Education Association.

Paludi, M., 1991. *Ivory Power: Sexual Harassment on Campus.* State University of New York Press.

Sexual Harassment: Suggested Policy and Procedures for Handling Complaints. 1995. In Policy Documents and Reports: American Association of University Professors.

Physical Disabilities and Learning Disabilities

Kathleen Schatzberg, Cape Cod Community College

118

*Resource
Handbook
for
Academic
Deans*

Providing accommodations for students with disabilities should not be a new endeavor. Recent publicity concerning the Americans with Disabilities Act (ADA) has brought additional attention to the issue, but most colleges and universities have been subject to similar requirements for more than two decades under the provisions of Section 504 of the Vocational Rehabilitation Act of 1973 which required any institution receiving federal funds to provide reasonable accommodations for persons with disabilities.

This requirement applies to every aspect of the institution, every constituency, every employee, every student, every user of the services and facilities. For the purposes of this handbook, we will assume that the entire college has implemented a comprehensive plan to address the mandate of ADA and proceed to address those concerns which relate specifically to instruction.

As chief academic officer, you must insure that well-publicized procedures are in place by which students may request reasonable accommodations. In many institutions, these procedures are established collaboratively with the chief student affairs officer. Indeed, many students have been so well-schooled at earlier stages of their education to identify their needs and advocate for themselves that they will announce their needs in the course of their application, and they may base their acceptance of an offer of admission upon their perception of how well the college responds to the needs of students with disabilities. Typically, student affairs staff will collect necessary documentation and advise the student on how to access services and obtain needed accommodations.

The most important role of the academic dean is to ensure that a welcoming and cooperative climate meets students with disabilities when they interact with faculty and engage their course work. You must be a role model in establishing the fact that students with disabilities enrich the experience of everyone in the learning community. Both the letter and the spirit of the law demand that reasonable accommodations be provided in order to insure access to education by persons with disabilities. You may encounter some resistance to this by some faculty or staff who may view accommodations as "special treatment" or a "watering down" of academic requirements. Such individuals must be persuaded that, in fact, reasonable accommodations are necessary to enable people with disabilities to be successful in meeting (not evading) the academic requirements of their chosen program of study.

Some court decisions over the years since Section 504 have established that colleges may deny access to certain kinds of programs when it can be demonstrated that the student's disability would result in danger to themselves or others. For instance, a student with narcolepsy was denied entrance to a culinary program on the basis that falling asleep while operating electric slicers or other kitchen equipment could easily lead to serious injury. Likewise, a student who depended upon lip-reading was denied access to a nursing program because of its required surgical rotation where the use of surgical masks might lead to communication deficits that could harm a patient. These extreme examples aside, students with disabilities must be granted access to the academic programs of their choice. It is obvious, then, that in the liberal arts and sciences, there could be almost no justification to deny a student access. Rather, the critical element is creativity in designing or modifying the learning experience so that a

student with disabilities has the same opportunity to achieve the same competencies as any other student.

The specific accommodations to be made are, of course, highly individualized to each student and each course. Working with academic support staff and the disabilities specialist on campus, the dean can ensure that faculty get the assistance they need to respond to each student's needs. Many colleges find it useful to provide staff development workshops on the law, on designing reasonable accommodations, and on the particular academic issues encountered with particular types of disabilities. Beyond that, each student's needs must be handled on a case-by-case basis, so that the disabilities specialist serves not only the advocacy role for students but also a role as support for faculty as they work to design needed accommodations. Tutoring, extended time for examinations, oral examinations, and dictation of papers are all fairly simple to accomplish. More complex might be training a teacher in classroom teaching style that will accommodate a student who needs to use lip-reading or assisting a science lab instructor in modifying lab experiences to accommodate a student who is blind or confined to a wheelchair. The very heart of providing accommodations, however, begins with the commitment to provide access to students with disabilities. Assuming that commitment, the rest is relatively easy.

Another aspect of accommodating students with disabilities that will concern you is budgeting. Within the academic realm of the college, most accommodative services are relatively low-cost. Extra time for exams costs almost nothing—existing staff in tutoring centers or the faculty member themselves can provide proctoring. Tutoring for disabled students costs no more than tutoring for any other student, and most colleges now provide tutoring services that are available for any student who wants to use the service. Books on tape are provided to people with visual disabilities at no cost to the college, provided textbooks are identified early enough to allow for taping. Some kinds of accommodation are costly, however, and these costs must be planned for and built into the budget. Providing signers for deaf students, for instance, can be a substantial expense. The need to plan for such expenses makes it critical that students be encouraged to make their needs known early in the application process, and thereafter, to begin the registration process for each term as early as possible.

120

*Resource
Handbook
for
Academic
Deans*

Learning disabilities present some particular challenges for the academic dean. Faculty are more likely to be skeptical of the authenticity of learning disabilities. Intensive effort is usually required first, to help faculty understand learning disabilities and second, to reassure faculty that the institution collects appropriate documentation to verify the need for particular accommodations. A simple working definition should emphasize the fact that students with learning disabilities have normal or above average intelligence but have difficulty with processing information that may affect reading, listening, writing, speaking, or organizational abilities. Since learning disability is really an umbrella term covering many kinds of disability, accommodations are therefore highly individualized.

In this area more than any other, the college needs a disabilities specialist who can command the respect and trust of faculty. Ultimately, however, if some faculty continue to resist the authenticity of a documented learning disability, your intervention may be required to explain that the college's obligation to comply with the law cannot be compromised. In an increasingly litigious society, people with disabilities are learning that courtrooms may be an effective way to overcome the resistance of those who are not cooperative in providing necessary accommodations. You have an obligation, of course, to protect the institution to whatever extent possible from the expense of litigation and its potential for a tarnished reputation. Providing adequate professional development for faculty, establishing timely mechanisms for documenting disabilities and negotiating accommodations, and putting in place procedures by which students can access these services are all ways in which you can not only protect the college but build its good name as an institution that readily accommodates people with disabilities.

Throughout the entire process, from establishing policy and procedures, to providing professional development for faculty and staff, to meeting, greeting and working with students, the entire college community is well-served if certain general principles frame our responses to issues of disability. First, we welcome students with disabilities to our learning community because they help all of us, but most especially all students, to learn how to work in the real world of diverse humanity. Second, providing accommodations for students (and staff) with disabilities is everyone's job. The campus disabilities specialist may provide leadership and expertise, but everyone from president and dean to faculty and support staff are charged with the responsibility for making the campus one that enthusiastically welcomes students with disabilities and responds creatively to their needs. Finally, any costs in time and resources are well worth the opportunity that students with disabilities provide us for living our commitment to the humane goals of a liberal arts education.

6

The Financial Side of Deaning

ACAD

AMERICAN CONFERENCE
OF ACADEMIC DEANS

STRATEGIC PLANNING

David E. Leary, University of Richmond

Unless an institution is to change willy-nilly, without clear direction or purpose, its members should engage in some form of planning. To bemost effective, this planning should involve everyone who will be affected by its results, and it should be rooted in a strong sense of the institution's mission, history, and values. In its simplest formulation, "strategic planning," as it is commonly called these days, involves the clarification of goals, means, assessment, and resources.

GOALS

The best scenario for strategic planning begins with an entire institution. Any discussion of more specific goals—for instance, the goals of a School of Arts and Sciences—should take place within a clear understanding of the overall mission of the institution. Once determined, the institution's mission statement should provide the framework within which specific goals

are selected, articulated, and prioritized. Specific goals that do not contribute toward the fulfillment of the institution's mission should be dropped, or at least given a much lower priority in terms of the time, effort, and resources devoted to them. Without vigilance in this regard, planning will be "non-strategic" and relatively irrelevant to the on-going development of the institution.

When planning is initiated at a lower level within the institutional structure, without the benefit of a clearly defined institutional mission, initial efforts should be directed to the definition of the most general goals that can be agreed upon by the relevant participants. Once defined, they should be shared with those "higher up," with a request for feedback, so that these individuals—their insights and their cooperation—will be drawn into the planning process. Hopefully, this will help them "buy into" the results of the process.

Considering and debating alternative goals, with the objective of coming up with a relatively small number of common aims, is the core of any planning process. Besides preparing the way for an efficient and effective orchestration of community effort, the process of coming to communal agreement about a common set of goals is one of the best ways to *form* a community, i.e., a group of individuals sharing common aspirations, values, and objectives. In many ways, this is the most important stage in the planning process. It shouldn't go on forever, but it shouldn't be fore-shortened before everyone has a chance to have his or her say, or before the group reaches a reasonable consensus. The process should *engage* rather than *disengage* its participants. This doesn't mean that tough decisions do not have to be made; sometimes they do, and sometimes they will disappoint some individuals. But the process should be open and fair: All points of view should be allowed expression; all reactions should be made public. Learning to deal "up front" with differences of opinion—valuing and yet discriminating among them—is one of the key ingredients and benefits of a planning process. Decisions must be made in establishing goals and in putting them into practice; the sooner the group takes responsibility for making such decisions, the sooner planning will become a valued component in the community's life.

There are many things that can be considered as a community tries to clarify its primary goals. Besides their institution's basic mission, which generally takes into account their institution's history, traditions, values, and constituents, many planning groups find it useful to take a

"SWOT" approach at a rather early stage. This acronym stands for Strengths, Weaknesses, Opportunities, and Threats:

❖ What are the relative strengths and weaknesses of the institution, of its faculty, students, majors, and programs, of its relevant facilities and resources, etc.?

❖ What opportunities are opening up, or will soon open up, because of changes in personnel, environment, job market, etc.?

To answer these and other related questions, it is generally helpful to get some "internal" and "external" data. External data from other institutions will provide "benchmarks" or comparisons that will ground the assessment of strengths and weaknesses in fact rather than fiction. In addition, finding out what similar institutions are doing, what they have accomplished with similar students or resources, how their students are faring after graduation, etc., can be a good source of ideas and insight, though it is good *not* to import external goals and programs without appropriate modifications. Every institution and every community is different and has its own particular potentials. Simply copying some other institution or community is not likely to lead to the kind of self-determined directionality that bodes best for the future. Communities that have learned to think and act for themselves are in the best position to take advantage of their own distinctive opportunities.

In the end, this primary phase in strategic planning should help create or renovate a community of enthusiastic, motivated *believers*, individuals who share a common commitment to a vision which they have helped to create, which is appropriate for their institution, and which has a realistic chance of coming to fruition. Reaching beyond one's current grasp is the name of the game; reaching too far, beyond all realistic expectation, is a formula for discouragement. Since some individuals will drop out of the process at the first signs of discouragement, it is important to orchestrate a sequential implementation pattern that will optimize early successes and establish an expectation of continued successful development. The *process* of continued participation and positive achievements is more important, in many ways, than the *end products* themselves. The thought that I keep in mind is: I would rather get "there" in five years with everyone on Board, than in one year with half the people overboard. Pyrrhic victories leave no one satisfied.

MEANS

The best goals in the world mean nothing if you don't have the means of realizing them. A key component in strategic planning is the determination of how the group (whether at the university, school, or department level) is going to try to reach its goals. Any plan should specify how this is to be done. (The language of strategic planning is often confusing and distinguishing. For example, in some cases between *goals*, *objectives*, and *action*, goals being general, objectives being the means toward particular goals, and actions being the very specific ways in which objectives will be met. But at bottom we are talking common sense here. You need to clarify how you are going to get from *where you are* to *where you want to be.* Create your own language, if it is more useful to you.)

Again, the means that are chosen to accomplish any goal could be borrowed and adapted from some other institution, or from some other unit in your own institution. But whether inspired by other groups or not, these means have to be "owned" by the planning group—at least articulated in their own way, for their own specific purpose. Unless they fully accept particular objectives and actions, they are unlikely to follow through on them over time. This is where deans are often challenged. You may see relative weaknesses in the implementation strategies of a group, and may wish (and may be able) to influence their revision. But to *order* certain changes is not a recipe for success. Working with units, helping them monitor feedback, taking a progressive on-going revision approach seems, generally, the best way for you to proceed. Unless, of course, the performance of a particular unit is so poor that more radical intervention is necessary. This would constitute a special case, however; the exception should not determine the rule. In most institutions, there are enough people of good will and sufficient talent to warrant a more patient, continual improvement approach to the implementation of strategic plans.

In developing concrete strategies for reaching their goals, it is often very helpful for units, whether schools or departments, to bring in some external consultants. In my experience, the results of consultation are best when the unit has already articulated a draft of its goals and has at least a tentative list of means for reaching these goals. This establishes the fact that consultants are not being brought in to do the work of the unit, but to provide meaningful feedback on their work. In addition, I have found it useful to bring in two consultants rather than one, and to have each consultant submit a separate written report after the campus visit. (Prior to the visit, these consultants are sent copies of the unit's plan and as much relevant data on the unit, its faculty, its programs, its students, its graduates, etc., as possible. During the visit, they meet with faculty, students, and administrators, and review as representative a sample of student work as can be made available to them. In many cases, of course, strategic planning *calls for* the collection of student work that is not yet available in meaningful quantity and variety. But in subsequent rounds of planning, which at my institution are now slated for every 5-7 years, more adequate representations of student work will be available.) The submission of two external consultant reports underscores that there is no one "external view" of the unit, that the diverse views of the consultants are to be taken seriously but not unduly privileged. Of course, when both consultants agree on something, this puts an additional onus on the unit to explain why they did not accept a particular recommendation, if in fact they decide not to do so.

ASSESSMENT

Once a unit decides upon particular goals and means, it makes sense to ask how the members of the unit will know whether or not they are making good progress toward these goals, how they will know whether or not the means they have chosen are proving to be adequate, and how they will know what modifications to make in order to facilitate a more timely achievement of their goals. This is what assessment is all

about, and I find that faculty (who in some cases may resist evaluation and assessment) are easily persuaded that it makes sense to monitor their progress toward their goals *so that their time and efforts will not be wasted.* How their progress is to be monitored, whether by quantitative or qualitative means, or both, is largely a function, I believe, of the nature of their goals, the kinds of information that would be relevant to them, and their own methodological and conceptual dexterity.

Again, it is critical that the *process* of assessment be owned and operated, to the fullest possible extent, by the members of the unit. Once units see that the intent is not to judge their failures but to help them achieve their own common goals, they generally come to accept and even embrace ongoing self-assessment, both as a group and as individuals. Clearly, a light but firm touch "from above" will help here and there, but it is often sufficient simply to make it clear that you, as dean, value what they are doing and stand ready to review what they are doing with them. In addition, of course, it helps to build an annual assessment section into the annual review report that most units are expected to submit. These annual assessment reports should demonstrate progressive development over time. In particular, they should demonstrate how the unit is *using* the results of assessment, whatever form those results may take. "Closing the loop" in assessment—using the results to make midcourse corrections in order to optimize progress toward goals—is the critical matter. Again, faculty come to understand this as they begin to see the positive outcome of the planning- action-assessment-revision cycle.

The main trick is to encourage a unit to find the most meaningful-and-cost-effective way of doing assessment. Faculty are busy; they have lots to do; they hate to feel that something is a waste of time. Only if certain results will *mean* anything to them—will *persuade* them to do something differently—should they be collected. The collection of data that means something to people in other units, or in other institutions, but not to the members of the unit that is gathering them, is just out-and-out stupid. Challenge the members of your units to arrive at a consensus about what set of data would be the most useful to them, the most significant in relation to their goals and to the value system that facilitated the articulation of these goals. If having a direct conversation with all graduating seniors promises to be more meaningful than the results of umpteen standardized, nationally normed tests, then buy a coffee machine and reserve a lounge for lots of conversations!

The goal of assessment is improvement. Improvement will occur only if the principals are persuaded by the results of assessment. Although your faculty may be different from mine, I suggest that you ask them to keep their assessment program as meaningful and as simple as possible. Since any given assessment technique can give a distorted perspective, this does not mean that they should decide upon only one means of assessment. Multiple means are always preferable, but each of the multiple means should be meaningful and cost-effective.

Some of the assessment procedures that my institution's units have found useful, in addition to teaching evaluations and external reviews, are exit interviews with graduating seniors, blind reviews of student papers, data on post-graduate schooling and employment, feedback from graduate-program advisers and employers, comparisons of data and practice with nationally prominent units in other institutions, analysis of the characteristics, knowledge, and skills of in-coming students in relation to those of graduating seniors, and tracking of the progress of individual students through student portfolios. The hope, as I have said, is for "continuous improvement," but my experience suggests that it is a mistake to use jargon, much less acronyms like TQM, to convey the common-sense objective of getting better each and every day (or at least each and every year). Try to keep your people focused on what can be achieved, not on their relative weaknesses or failures. No one likes to fall short; all of us enjoy being part of a winning effort.

RESOURCES

My own philosophy is that, in order to get better, institutions (and the units within them) need *vision, will,* and *resources*—in that order. Defining a mission and common goals is how a community creates a vision that will elicit sufficient motivation and effort to transform hopes into reality. Much can be accomplished with vision and will alone, and we all know examples of individuals and institutions achieving far beyond their apparent resources. Money alone (to pick only one kind of resource) will not create a good institution or a strong unit. However, certain goals, certain means, and certain ways of monitoring progress toward a realizable vision can be achieved only with a certain amount of resources. The resource question should come last, after goals, means, and a monitoring system have been determined; but though it should come last, it is still vitally important. (Of course, this is too simple: you need to have a good idea of *possible* resources as you plan your goals, means, and assessment procedures. But plenty of good opportunities have been lost by groups that do not set their goals high enough because they are prematurely certain that they cannot muster the resources to achieve them.)

Timing is important, and so are credibility and incentive. To insure that the units within my own School of Arts and Sciences would initiate planning when it was best for them, I announced seven years ago (after our institution as a whole had completed a University-level strategic plan) that I expected each unit to have completed a strategic plan at least by the next visit of our accreditation association (i.e., within seven years), but that I realized that each individual unit would want to schedule its own planning process (within this seven years) in light of its own particular situation (e.g., its last planning phase, upcoming sabbaticals, expected retirements and hirings, etc.). I also underscored that I did not want to waste anyone's time, so I wanted as succinct a strategic plan as possible, provided that it specified goals, means, assessment, and resources. To give the process credibility and to provide some incentive, I announced that those units that completed their plans first would be at the front of the line in terms of allocation of resources. For instance, I emphasized that future hiring and funding decisions would take strategic plans into serious consideration.

This did *not* mean that departments could expect anything or everything they wished. It meant that their arguments for particular things would be significantly enhanced if they could show that these things were essential components in a thoughtful and persuasive plan that was consonant with the institution's general mission and goals.

Institutions of higher learning are notoriously short of resources these days, but even so, strategic planning can help insure that those resources, however limited, are used to best effect. Even if new resources are available, either through institutional sources or through external fund raising, reallocation of existing resources will almost certainly become a necessary part of any significant forward movement within higher education settings. Such reallocation—whether of staffing, operating costs, capital expenditure funds, or whatever—will create understandable concerns among faculty. The best I can suggest is that the more public and the more widely agreed-upon are the goals to be served by the reallocation of resources, the easier it will be for members of the community to accept, and even applaud, this reallocation. Of course, this is said by a dean who has been extremely fortunate in being at an institution with a considerable resource base. I will leave it to others to provide more specific advice regarding how best to operate under more stringent circumstances, but I suspect that the same general principle will remain in effect.

As regards the important question of how you can compete effectively for resources within the larger institution, it seems clear that it is helpful, when making an argument for enhanced resources, to relate the need for them to a clearly defined set of commonly agreed-upon goals. Everyone wants more faculty, higher budgets, better equipment. But what *specific* outcomes, related to what goals, having what sort of impact on the fulfillment of the institution's mission, can you promise—or at least point out as probable—if you are given additional resources? Strategic planning can be, and should be, one of most effective means of insuring a fair, equitable, and appropriate distribution of resources. For this reason as well as for what it promises in terms of purposeful development, the engagement of the community, and hope for the future, it would be wise for you to argue for strategic planning if your institution does not already sponsor it, and to support its processes and ends to the fullest possible extent. Not for its own sake, not because it is currently fashionable, but because it is the smart and right thing to do.

FUND ACCOUNTING

Douglas Steeples, Mercer University

132

*Resource
Handbook
for
Academic
Deans*

You may already have discovered that charitable, not-for-profit entities maintain their financial records differently than do for-profit enterprises. These differences reflect the special needs of the former, which have resulted in the development of distinctive practices and accounting standards. However, in both the for-profit and the not-for-profit sectors, entities usually keep their records on an accrual basis. That is, they account for revenues in the period in which they are earned, and expenses in the period in which they are incurred, even though cash payments of those revenues and expenses may occur at some later period.

The best way to highlight differences between accrual accounting of for-profits and the practices of not-for-profits is to compare simplified balance sheets for the two types of entities.

In every solvent entity, whether for-profit or not-for-profit, the annual financial statement displays a balance between assets and liabilities (or their not-for-profit equivalents), and operating results are shown in terms of profits or losses, or positive or negative (results) or variances (from budget). For-profit entities usually employ the calendar year as their fiscal year. In higher education, the most common fiscal year is July 1-June 30.

In the case of a for-profit, the sources of assets are sales of shares of ownership (usually through stock), sales of goods and services, and borrowing. The situation is more complicated for a not-for-profit. There are no sales of shares of ownership in not-for-profits, hence no stocks or other forms of paid-in capital (equities) to account for, although there might well be borrowing. There are no earnings (hence no retained earnings), although there are operating results for which to account. And there are numerous sources of funds other than through borrowing, and through the sale of goods and services. These sources may include gifts, bequests, grants in response to proposals specifying

The balance sheet of a for-profit might look pretty much like this:

AJAX PROFIT COMPANY BALANCE SHEET, DECEMBER 31, 1996 ($000s)

ASSETS		LIABILITIES AND EQUITIES	
Current Assets		Current Liabilities	
Cash	$1,000	Accounts Payable	$2,100
Marketable Securities	1,000	Bank Loans payable	250
Accts. Receivable	3,675	Accrued Liabilities	490
Inventories	6,850	Est. Tax Liability	825
Prepaid Expenses	360	Current Portion of Long-term Dept	500
Total Current Assets	**$ 13,135**	**Total Current Liabilities**	**$4,165**
Noncurrent Assets		**Noncurrent Liabilities**	
Property, Plant, Eq.		Long-term Debt, less current	
Cost	$14,600	Portion	$1,500
Accumulated Depreciation	7,300	Deferred Income Taxes	650
Property, Plant, Eq. Net	7,300		
Investments	780	Total Liabilities	$6,315
Patents and Trademarks	260		
Goodwill	650	Equities	
Total Noncurrent, Net	$8,990	Common Stock	$2,000
		Other Paid-in Capital	$3,000
		Total, Paid-in Capital	$5,000
		Retained Earnings	**$10,810**
Total Assets	**$22,125**	**Total Liabilities and Equities**	**$22,125**

*The
Financial
Side of
Deaning*

intended uses, and legislative enactaments making funds available for designated uses.

Revenues from sales of goods and services and gifts and grants for which no purpose is specified may be used at the discretion of the entity. Their use is, then, denominated as "unrestricted." Revenues from donors, granting agencies, lenders, and legislatures that specify their intended uses may be deployed only as their sources prescribe. Such revenues are termed "restricted," although their sources may stipulate either current or capital

purposes. Management of restricted funds is explicitly a trust responsibility of the governing board of a not-for-profit entity, since the entity has been incorporated under state laws governing the formation of charitable organizations to serve specified public interests or purposes. In a sense, the management of unrestricted revenues is also a trust responsibility of the governing board, since that management must be prudent and must avoid incurring obligations that invade restricted revenues or that jeopardize the solvency of the entity and thereby threaten to invade restricted revenues and/or, of course, endowments.

The system of accounting that has developed to meet the needs of not-for-profit entities is called "Fund Accounting." The balance sheets for not-for-profit entities report through a system in which related activities are grouped together in categories called "funds." All income is allocated to appropriate funds, and all expenses are charged to appropriate funds. Fund Accounting replaces the equation employed in for-profits—**assets=liabilities+ equities**—with a new equation—**assets= liabilities+fund balances**. It is to the fund balances that we should direct our attention if we are interested in the health of a not-for-profit entity, while observing movements and relationships across the balance sheet. The balances reflect the equivalent of retained earnings and equities.

Just as resources coming to a college or university may be designated unrestricted or restricted, so are the funds to which they flow. The usual fund groups are "Current," from which most operations are usually conducted; "Plant," where transactions involving land, buildings, and equipment are reflected; "Endowment," representing gifts held in trust by the entity the earnings of which support various aspects of the operation as may have been designated by donors; "Loan" funds, in the event that the institution lends resources; and "Agency" funds, where an institution accounts for any funds it holds for other bodies, such as student organizations, booster clubs, and the like.

Where there are excess unrestricted dollars available, a governing board may, at its discretion, move these dollars from one fund to another. Such an action is called a "nonmandatory transfer." There are also "mandatory transfers." These occur because all receipts are ordinarily recorded, initially, in the current fund. When the terms of receipt require allocation for particular purposes, these funds must be transferred per the governing terms. Most mandatory transfers result from contractual agreements that may contain provisions for payments to qualify for debt financing and loan programs. It is a common and sound practice of governing boards to allocate bequests that do not specify a use ("undesignated bequests") to investment, in order to earn income for a college or university. Funds so deployed are reflected under the fund group, "Endowment and Similar Funds." They are usually called "funds functioning as endowment," or "quasi-endowment," because, unlike true endowment which by terms of gift or bequest can be used for no other purposes, they can be transferred out of the investment pool and used for some other purpose at the discretion of the governing board.

You will find in associated reports—the Statement of Changes in Fund Balances; and the Statement of Current Fund Revenues, Expenditures, and Other Charges— entries consistent with fund accounting practices. As you turn to the annual budget, the same account groups may appear. But the annual budget, in dealing with receipts and expenses, will introduce additional categories that may be unfamiliar.

The most important source of operating revenue for private or independent colleges and universities is tuition and fees. While most public institutions are "formula-

134

Resource Handbook for Academic Deans

The following shows what a much-simplified university balance sheet might look like.

ZENITH UNIVERSITY BALANCE SHEET, 30 JUNE, 1996 ($000s)

ASSETS			LIABILITIES & FUND BALANCES		
	Current Year	Prior Year		Current Year	Prior Year
CURRENT FUNDS			**CURRENT FUNDS**		
Unrestricted			Unrestricted		
Cash	200	100	Accts. Payable	175	100
Investments	350	250	Accrued Liab	20	15
Accts. Receivable	380	200	Due to other Fund	160	110
Inventories at Cost (FIFO)	70	50	Fund Balance	705	385
Prepaid Expenses	10	20			
Total	1,010	620	Total	1,010	620
Restricted			Restricted		
Cash	90	80	Accts. Payable	20	5
Investments	150	140			
Accts. Receivable	70	90	Fund Balance	290	305
Total	310	310	Total	310	310
Total Current	**1,320**	**1,320**	**Total Current**	**1,320**	**930**
LOAN FUNDS			**LOAN FUNDS**		
			Fund Balances		
Cash	30	20	US Govt. Grants	30	20
Investments	50	60	Unrestricted Univ.	300	250
Loans	350	270	Restricted Univ.	100	80
Total Loans	**430**	**350**	**Total Loans**	**430**	**350**
ENDOWMENT AND SIMILAR FUNDS			**ENDOWMENT AND SIMILAR FUNDS**		
			Fund Balances		
Cash	20	20	Endowments	3,550	2,850
Investments	5,480	4,480	Quasi, unrestr.	1,050	950
			Quasi, restr.	900	700
Total Endow	5,500	4,500	Total Endow	5,500	4,500
PLANT FUNDS			**PLANT FUNDS**		
Unexpended			Unexpended		
Cash	350	570	Accts. Payable	100	150
Investments	1,250	1,500	Notes Payable	70	270
Due current unrestr.	160	110	Bonds Payable	1,100	1,300
			Fund bal., unrest.	390	260
			Fund bal., rest.	100	100
Total	**1,760**	**2,180**	**Total**	**1,760**	**2,180**
Retirement of Debt			Retirement of Debt		
Cash	10	10	Fund bal., unrestr.	10	10
Deposits w/trustees	250	450	Fund bal., restr.	250	450
Total	260	460	Total	260	460
Investment in Plant			Investment in Plant		
Land & Improvments	1,000	1,000	Notes Payable	350	350
Buildings	10,620	10,000	Bonds Payable	2,000	2,000
Equipment	1,000	1,000	Net Investment		
Library Collection	1,080	1,000	in Plant	11,350	10,650
Total	13,700	13,000	Total	13,700	13,000
Total Plant Funds	**15,720**	**15,640**	**Total Plant Funds**	**15,720**	**15,640**
AGENCY FUNDS			**AGENCY FUNDS**		
Cash	5		Fund Balance	5	
TOTAL	**22,975**	**21,420**	**TOTAL**	**22,975**	**21,420**

funded" (the amount legislatively appropriated bears some prescribed relationship to enrollment), tuition and fees are assuming increasing importance in state-assisted (public) colleges and universities as well. The greater the role of these sources of revenue, the more "tuition dependent" or "enrollment driven" an institution is said to be. The prevailing view is that somewhere on the order of 65-80% of the operating income for educational and general expenditures of a private institution ought to come from tuition and fees.

"Auxiliary Services," which typically include the operation of and revenues from the residence halls, bookstore, food service, and the like, would, depending on the relative importance of a resident student body, perhaps generate as much as 30% or more of the total institutional budget. For residential campuses, the goal of a 10% net return from auxiliary services with which to subsidize the educational and general budget, is common.

In the private sector, a common aspiration is for endowment and funds functioning as endowment to provide, through a combination of earnings and capital gains, from 10 to 25% of the educational and general budget, although a great many institutions find this an unattainable goal. State appropriations may serve as a comparable source of funding in the public sector. Gifts and grants, in either event, are often required to achieve a balanced budget.

When we turn from financial statements to the budget, we find that our operating charges (generally charged against the current fund) fall into several key categories. These are:

Resource Handbook for Academic Deans

Educational and General—the largest, containing expenditures for

❖ Instruction (normally 27-35% of Educational & General)
❖ Research
❖ Public Service
❖ Academic Support (Library, academic administration, etc.)
❖ Institutional Support (governing board, president, business affairs, advancement, purchasing, human resources, etc.)
❖ Operation and Maintenance of Plant
❖ Scholarships/Financial Aid
❖ Mandatory Transfers for
   ◆ Principal and Interest
   ◆ Renewals and Replacements
   ◆ Loan Fund Matching
   ◆ Grant Matches
❖ Total Expenditures and Mandatory Transfers, Educational and General

Auxiliary Enterprises
❖ Expenditures
❖ Mandatory Transfers for
   ◆ Principal and Interest
   ◆ Renewals and Replacements
❖ Total Expenditures and Mandatory Transfers for Auxiliary Services

Other Transfers and Additions
❖ Excess of restricted receipts over transfers to revenues
❖ Refunded to grantors
❖ Unrestricted gifts allocated to other funds
❖ Portion of quasi-endowment gains appropriated
❖ Net increase in fund balance.

SOME CAUTIONARY OBSERVATIONS

Anyone who has shared in many accreditation visits or enjoyed extensive administrative experience will appreciate that fund accounting, like its counterpart in the for-profit sector, can conceal as much as it reveals. Persons who are candidates for deanships or new to administration are well advised to recall the admonition, *caveat emptor*. A candidate, or a new dean, who neglects to ask for, and review, the most recent two or three years' worth of audited financial statements for an institution, is inviting unpleasant surprises. Financial statements can provide indications of fiscal problems, or the threat of fiscal problems.

Suppose, for example, that Zenith University's Unrestricted Current Funds included cash of $800,000, while the Plant Fund, Endowment, or Quasi-Endowment carried a notation "Due from Current Fund," $1,000,000. Such entries would replace a positive cash balance with a negative balance in the current fund of $200,000 and would reflect interfund borrowing. While interfund borrowing can be a legitimate means of meeting short-term liquidity needs, it can also indicate a serious shortage of resources with which to meet obligations. Or the statement could show that there were no funds functioning as endowment, meaning that the entire quasi-endowment (if there had ever been one) had been spent down. Or it could reflect sums due to the endowment itself, indicating borrowing from the endowment.

One might also encounter entries for any of these funds contained within parentheses, indicating negative balances. At least one college has in recent years deeded its campus over to the city in which it is situated, so that the city would pick up debts standing against the campus. Then it used its endowment to purchase the campus back at a somewhat discounted price. The transaction was represented as a productive investment of endowment on grounds that the institution could not do business without a campus, even though the transaction carried no promise of a return on the purported investment.

Either as a candidate or a newly appointed dean, you need at the very least to assess two other indices of institutional fiscal strength, through an examination of financial statements. One is the "current ratio": the ratio of 90-day receivables to 90-day payables, as well as of current year receivables to payables. The other is the "discount rate": net tuition dollars received as opposed to the nominal tuition rate. The conventional wisdom has been that a discount rate of 15-20% could be optimal. Market pressures, however, have driven the rate up rapidly, to the point that many institutions are near or at 30%, and some are above 40%. Discovery of adverse trends in either of these indices should induce caution, if not serious concern.

Special Budgets

Gary L. Maris, Stetson University

MANAGING GRANTS

Grant approval process. It is important for you to have a good grant approval process at your college or university. This should be *simple* and involve one to two pages of basic information, determining:

1. Basic intent of the grant
2. Any college commitments
3. From whom it will be requested (This avoids different grant request conflicting. Also, you may wish to use a particular strategy in seeking grants from particular foundations or government agents.)
4. Any effect on curriculum of the grant
5. Any effect on faculty staffing
6. A budget (This needs to indicate all revenues expected from granting agency and all expenses expected by the college, including in-kind commitments.)

7. The possibility of hiring adjuncts for release time grants and the effect on the curriculum
8. Matching grants and the college commitment (This is particularly the case with the NSF equipment grants. Ideally, it's good to have a capital pool where money is available for any matching funds. However, this often is not the case. This means having to identify the source of the matching funds ahead of time. In some rare instances, several faculty may apply for these grants and success may mean a rather large matching grants bill for the college.)

Daily managing. Usually grants are managed by two persons—the person who is requesting the grant and a person in the finance office. The financial person should be able to set up the account and manage the expenditures and financial reports, thus freeing the faculty member of this onerous, and sometimes complicated and technical, task. The faculty member will have the responsibility of seeing to the proper expenditure of the grant. Your role is to ensure that all is being done properly; normally, however, the faculty member receiving the grant will conscientiously and scrupulously adhere to the various terms of the grant.

SPECIAL ENDOWMENT BUDGETS

Some departments tend to squirrel away restricted funds, as though the funds were an end in themselves. You need to be sure that these funds are, in timely fashion, going to be put to use in support of research and teaching. One way to end this squirreling habit is for you to indicate to departments that they need to "use 'em or lose 'em." This can be done even if these are restricted funds by indicating that the funds will be used toward the departmental budgets if the department can find no other use for them. However, you must be careful in doing this lest the advantage of building up a fund for major usage has to be forgone in an attempt to spend money every year.

It's good to require annual budgets from the department with regard to any restricted funds for which it is responsible, and annual reports from your office or the financial officer regarding the status of these funds. Restricted funds can actually get lost or forgotten when a leadership shift occurs the department and the former chair fails to write anything down about the grant, and no reports are issued either from or to the department.

Communication between the college office raising funds and the academic departments and yourself is needed. Some funds may have come into a college and simply been placed into a restricted account without adequate information to the department or the dean's office. This may mean no one in the academic area is aware that the funds even exist. Yes, this has happened. You need to make sure that it won't happen at your institution.

What are "restrictions?" Often great latitude is provided to departments receiving restricted funds. Usually the comptroller or such person tied closely to the auditing process will know the specific character of the conditions governing the use of any restricted fund. It is not uncommon that departments may be free to do many more things with their funds than they might imagine. However, there are some instances when the donor has tied the funds down so closely they can hardly be used. This is something to remember in raising funds or discussing restricted funds with donors. It's good to keep them restricted sufficiently so that indeed it is the department that receives these funds and they don't just end up as general income. But if restricted funds are too highly restricted, the department's hands are tied and the money may not be used for worthwhile educational purposes.

Some funds have particular sensitivities attached to them that need to be noted. For example, a donor may have provided the funds in memory of a son or daughter. To call the funds simply by the donor's last name may miss this point and not provide the recognition the donor desires. This seems like a minor item, but it happens and can affect a sizable amount of money. Be sensitive about such sensitivities, not only while seeking funds but also in expending them—and in your or the department's thank-you report to the donor.

Universities can "sweep" funds at times of financial emergencies, if the restrictions are general enough. They do this through the accounting procedure of indicating that the restricted funds are being used as the "first dollars" in meeting the budgets of the particular department to which the funds are directed. For example, restricted funds for the Department of Biology to use for enhancing its field study labs might be used simply against the basic laboratory budget. This obviously is not the intent of donors, but it is often technically possible and proper. It is nonetheless a rather pernicious, demoralizing practice that can kill the incentive for faculty members to raise funds and donors to give funds. This is one reason to be careful in the wording of restrictions so that they are tight enough to avoid general budget uses but broad enough to give the department latitude to use them effectively. Ideally, you should work toward practices that don't permit sweeping up such restricted funds even in times of economic challenge.

DEPARTMENTAL vs. POOLED BUDGETS

Some items naturally fit best simply within departments, e.g., office expenses. Some items may be either pooled or departmental or both. I shall focus on three sorts of funds in which a "pooled" approach sometimes makes sense. Generally speaking, pooled funds have the advantage of making better use of "excess" funds and so are most useful where a department's needs are likely to vary from year to year.

Travel funds. In the case of travel, a pooled approach would mean having travel funds available to distribute to those faculty members who frequently attend conferences and not having the funds tied up in departments where faculty members are less active. If travel is on a per-faculty-member basis, whereby each faculty member is provided a set amount of money to travel to professional conferences whether they are presenting papers or not, it can simply be left with the departments. These funds tend to be expended regularly and departmental management avoids the administrative process of having to filter everything through the dean's office for regular tasks. However, travel funds that are provided on the basis of the presentation of papers at conferences and other kinds of "on-program" functions may be kept or centralized, since this distribution will probably not be as widely dispersed in practice. It's not a bad idea to have a two-part system with:

1. An account in each department with a basic amount of money per faculty member for professional travel. This is simply for professional development.
2. A pooled amount for special travel requests beyond the basic amount. This would be restricted only to faculty presenting papers at conferences or having other active roles in the conferences which make it more special than simply attending conferences for professional development.

Computers/software. This is a good area for having pooled resources. It's best to have a coordinated, comprehensive college program for purchasing and distributing computer resources. This allows a better distribution of resources, since some departments may be more heavily into computer usage than other departments, and the multiple possibilities for different kinds of software and hardware necessitate some centralized decision-making process in order to avoid chaos. If each department has its own funds and makes autonomous decisions then departments with greater computer usage may have insufficient funding and departments that have very modest computer needs may have an excess of funding. It may also mean that departments will purchase types of hardware that the institution is unable to service, either because of insufficient parts or a lack of expertise.

You should be involved in determining priorities for distribution of computer resources, even though these may be coming out of a central office such as the Office of Information Technology. You have a good awareness of what is happening in the various departments (or should have!) and can better gauge the impact on the curriculum, the number of majors, and the work of particular faculty members than someone heading up an office of information technology. Pooled resources enable a college to capitalize on economy of scale and on-site licensing when purchasing computer resources. Sometimes a central buyer can even get some equipment "tossed in" due to the size of the purchase that is taking place. This would not usually be available to an individual department.

If funds are pooled with regard to computers and software, an academic committee on computers should be formed so that substantial academic input is in place. This committee should be representative of various segments of the university, from the philosophers to the number-crunching physicists and computer scientists. The various needs of different disciplines must have a chance to express themselves in the strategic decisions being made for the comprehensive expenditure in the computer science area.

Capital funds. Capital funds are best used as pooled funds, although there are occasional exceptions. Departments that tend to have major capital expenditures on a regular basis, such as those in the natural sciences, should have some basic capital funds available to them on an annual basis. However, in general it's best to hold capital funds in a pool in order to distribute resources in a more efficient fashion. Capital expenditures by their very nature have various years of obsolescence; therefore, not all departments are going to have major capital needs every year. Also, capital needs tend to be rather large items and are hard to manage if your budget is dispersed across all the various departments.

The allocation of capital resources is best done by allowing departments to provide annual lists of capital needs and to provide prioritization of these needs. This allows you to make a master list of capital needs and amounts, indicate departmental priorities, and indicate your priorities as dean. With the help of computer spreadsheets, it's easy to manipulate these lists so as to see how many first-priority needs can be met, etc. It also allows you to keep track of which departments are receiving capital funds and how well these funds are being distributed throughout the institution.

Maintenance funds. The reasoning that pertains to capital funds also applies here.

Discretionary funds. These are a luxury not often available to deans. However, in one college these discretionary funds have provided the dean with the leeway to make many people happy, often with small allocations. For example, the request for $200 to help a student attend a professional conference to present a paper in collaboration with a faculty member often is a morale booster to both. Likewise, the opportunity to help a department give $200 or $300 as an honorarium for a speaker in a particular discipline provides enrichment in that department's program for that year which may not be a regular occurrence. There are numerous and varied requests that come to deans that often amount to only a few hundred dollars. The more deans are able to say yes, the higher the morale in the college and the more good things take place. Since these are often somewhat haphazard depending upon particular students or faculty members or possibilities in any given year, having

pooled discretionary funds allows the flexibility to "go with the flow" of requests in any given year. Keeping track with a computer spreadsheet permits you to balance assistance to different departments and avoids a particularly aggressive department from obtaining a lion's share of the funds.

Critical to the use of pooled resources is:
1. Your willingness to prioritize needs/requests.
2. Your careful tracking of who is getting what, in order to see how widely distributed the funds are to various departments and persons.
3. Your tough skin for the barbs from departments and individuals when saying no. Clear reasons for priorities and a "fairness" in distribution will help lessen the criticism and increase understanding among those whose requests are denied.

DEALING WITH NEW TECHNOLOGY

Carol A. Lucey, Alfred State College of Technology

The use of technology in academic settings is becoming a hot topic whenever academics get together. Undergraduate instruction in areas such as communications, English, foreign language, mathematics, and the sciences are making greater and greater use of computers. National Science Foundation Instrumentation and Laboratory Improvement (ILI) funds are increasingly going to computer-based instruction projects. Librarians are changing the way they do business as a result of on-line search access. The whole education enterprise is changing character as a result of the Internet and video-conferencing. Many administrators now see technology use as a potential cost-cutting mechanism for dealing with such refractory problems as the high cost of instruction per FTE and high library periodical budgets. How effective is all this new technology in cutting costs and enhancing educational experiences and where is it all leading us? Below, I discuss budgeting for technology needs, planning, fairness across the curriculum, and consequences of technology use in instruction.

BUDGET AND PLANNING ISSUES

It is almost a cliche that the technology needs of a college expand to consume the funds available. Here are some clear caveats for the novice administrator moving into this area:

Planning

If your information technology services delivery department does not already have a college-wide steering board, form one immediately. This board should be composed of representatives of all areas of the college that use the department's services. Be sure to include such users as the registrar, institutional research, and the clerical staff, as well as the heavy academic users (these will probably include the library, the sciences, and perhaps the writing center and tutoring services area.) If students are assessed a technology fee, they should also have a representative, elected from some duly authorized organization such as a student senate.

The Infotech director or dean should chair the board. A board membership assignment should be viewed as high prestige (you might want the president to issue appointment letters each year to the board's members) and should meet frequently. Stick your nose into this area often to make sure they are meeting and that the information flow is from users to technology providers, not the other way around. All major upgrades that involve large investments of staff time should have broad support. "Migrations" in operating systems, which are almost always associated with major service dislocation and heavy costs, should be clearly understood and supported by the users before any decisions are made.

Technology budgets should, to the extent possible, be allocated by the steering board, not by the technical staff. Also, don't get trapped into making budget allocation decisions by yourself, unless you are willing to walk the plank when a major upgrade fails. And new technology often does fail!

Planning and "flashy new stuff":

There are some wonderful new toys on display at every technology trade show. Educom is one of the best, if you want to see technology in action in an academic setting. However, avoid the "bleeding edge." Get suspicious of requests to pur-

chase untried technology. Once your team and your board tell you they want to go forward with some new, flashy system, ask them to go visit a college with a working version. Go with them, if you can. Ask your counterpart at the other college questions such as: how many person hours did you spend to get this thing to run? How often does it go down? How much did you spend on hardware upgrades to make it work? How much support does your technical staff have to commit to this thing to keep it running? Do your students ever complain, and what about? And stay away from version 1.0 of anything.

Distance Learning

A special caveat on the video-based distance learning "bleeding edge": you will have trouble with the software, with the telephone service provider, with the video equipment, and with the computer. You will spend money on technicians who can never be far from the class when it is running. The system will "go down" at inopportune times during the semester, and you will have to have videotape backup available. Additionally, you will have all of these problems at the remote site.

You will spend more on your line charges, your technical support, and capital amortization than a "live" adjunct instructor would cost you. And the system will take you at least two semesters longer to get operational than promised. In the end, if you are breaking even on the cost of instruction, most of your students won't like it (you'll be "sending to" too many students at too many sites), your faculty will worry about workload issues, and parents will complain that this sort of instruction is not what they expected when they paid their student's tuition bill.

Despite all of the above, there is a place for distance learning technology in higher education. Isolated colleges who cannot hire qualified full time or adjunct instructors for exotic courses will find that they can enrich their students' curriculum by use of distance learning. In general, however, don't expect a bargain in this technology.

The Internet

If you have reasonably good "bandwidth" (i.e., a T1 or faster telephone connection) to the world of the Internet, spend some money on a good campus home page system. This can become the foundation of a college information service for your students, your faculty, your alumni, and your prospective students. It can also give you a jumping off point for some specialized "asynchronous learning" course work. This will probably be one of the most effective forms of technological delivery of new educational services in the future. The Alfred P. Sloan Foundation is now funding experimental projects to explore the use of this new medium.

Downloading costs

If your residence halls aren't currently "wired" to the campus backbone (i.e., the optical fiber infrastructure, over which the college network services are delivered), allocate some resources to do so immediately. Encouraging students to install their own computing equipment in their residence halls will make for happier users and will decrease some of the wear and

tear on college-owned machines. Eventually, this should allow you to diminish the size of the budget you have to spend on hardware which has a very short useful lifetime. Caveat: be prepared to offer some basic troubleshooting and some campus computer repair services. These can be outsourced, if you are not too far from a metropolitan area.

Many hardware and software vendors offer wonderful discounts to faculty and staff and students affiliated with higher education institutions. Ask your infotech dean or director to arrange a campus purchase plan through the college employees' credit union that will allow faculty and staff to purchase computers for themselves on time plans, taking advantage of these steep discounts. That will promote faculty and staff professional development and cost the college practically nothing!

Timing

Practice "just in time" principles on technology purchases. That is, don't buy more than your faculty and staff know how to use, and don't train your faculty and staff to use technology you're not prepared to deliver. The former will cost you money and cause underutilization and the latter will frustrate your faculty and staff and cause morale problems. Tailor your training to match your purchases.

In technology purchases, there is no such thing as a long-term investment. Whatever you do, don't buy more technology than you need at any given time, thinking you'll grow into it. Technology does not age well, and those are your precious equipment dollars sitting there in that large piece of high-tech junk! If you've got some end-of-the-year, extra cash to spend, always choose to spend it on faculty and staff professional development before turning it over to a technology committee for purchase of "toys."

"Hand-me-downs"

Avoid a campus "rolldown" policy. This occurs when the "innovators" and "early adopters" (usually in the sciences or technologies) always get the newest computers with the newest software versions, while the folks in areas defined as "nontechnical" always get stuck with the old machines when the early adopters abandon them. This ends up putting "286s" on the desks of the literature professors, because somebody decided they don't need anything but word processing. This will surely produce a morale problem in your literature department, and you won't have many literature professors ready or willing to try teaching via such new techniques as class on-line Lotus Notes conferencing or "asynchronous learning" on the Internet.

Having said all this, it is still necessary not to starve the creative early adopters of necessary new technology tools. Some colleges make a pool of competitive, "strategic initiative" grant funds available for use by such initiators. This money can then be used to fund new technology for the campus technology "spark plugs."

TECHNOLOGY AND THE CURRICULUM

Here are some things I've noticed about technology use in the classroom:

New technology as a catalyst

When science and math faculty decide to upgrade a course using interactive computing, the process is as important and as exciting for the instructor as it is for the student. Whole physics and mathematics departments have been revitalized by Priscilla Laws' "Workshop Physics" or by the Harvard Calculus program. These programs also encourage the use of "active learning" techniques by those faculty who are probably most prone to the "drink from the firehose" lecture technique.

Programs first

Be careful to make sure that your departments have done appropriate program planning before they make their technology purchases. The academic program should always dictate the purchase of the equipment type, not the other way around.

People first

Departments sometimes become so enamored of technology that they lose sight of the human dimension of what they are doing. Students do need instructors to set conceptual frameworks within which they can work before setting their classes to work on machines. Also, some students have a tough time breaking free from the traditional, nontechnological lecture format. Don't let the new technology delivery systems strip your curriculum of its humanity!

"On Stage"

Faculty love Powerpoint and similar presentation software packages. They are inexpensive and, with little effort, produce very elegant presentations that can incorporate videoclips and other multimedia materials. Take a large lecture room and turn it into a smart classroom with a computer, a good opaque overhead projector, and a high-quality projection system. You will quickly discover that faculty enjoy using this room for their courses. This kind of technology can produce a much better instructional experience in your large lecture sections for students and faculty alike.

Information Literacy and the Library

Be sure that your library is getting sufficient technology-based professional development funds, and don't shortchange them on equipment funds. All research projects today should include the use of search engines on the Internet as well as hard-copy library materials. Don't expect to save much yet on your periodicals budget, however. There are still too many copyright and cost issues unresolved and many professional society journals have therefore hesitated to go electronic, or they only permit access to users who also have hard-copy subscriptions.

Information vs. Transformation

Finally, many faculty worry about whether new technology, long-distance delivery, etc., will change the way they teach, or even render them irrelevant. The answer is probably different in different kinds of higher education enterprises. The lecture format of instruction is bound to become less viable as electronic media provide more alternatives for the simple conveyance of information. Many large universities are already moving to self-paced forms of technology-based instruction in place of experiences that used to occur in large lecture halls. Laboratory- and studio-dependent disciplines will probably not change much, except the equipment use will become more and more computer-based.

I am willing to bet that there will always be an important place for the small, personalized instruction format in undergraduate colleges. Perhaps new technology will serve its most useful purpose in the next few years by reinforcing the fact that most parents send their students to college for a transformational experience with other people. Those colleges with student-centered faculty and curriculums should survive the new technology.

Workload, Productivity, and Cost/Benefits

Myron S. Henry, University of Southern Mississippi

Since as dean you are probably accountable for major portions of the fiscal year budget of your institution, it is incumbent upon you to be knowledgeable about income generation and expenditures by units in the divisions you administer, as well as about other measures of unit or program productivity.

INCOME GENERATION, PROGRAM COSTS, AND SUPPORT FOR SERVICES

For most colleges and universities, academic programs consist of a series of interrelated courses (or learning experiences) taught or guided by faculty. From an assessment of learning perspective, an academic program might be judged as successful if students can demonstrate an appropriate level of new knowledge or skill attainment after having completed program requirements. This is an important measure of success. However, institutions must be able to "afford" to offer an array of academic programs appropriate to their mission. Therefore, *in the aggregate*, you need to weigh the benefits and costs of offering particular academic programs.

Direct costs to offer instructional programs certainly include compensation for "full-time equated faculty" (i.e., full-time faculty, "fractional faculty" determined from part-time instructional appointments, and graduate assistants) and support staff within academic units; current expenses (e.g., supplies, travel, phones, tuition waivers, and student employment within academic units); and instructional equipment. Costs incurred outside academic programs or units such as those for the library, heat, lights, cleaning, campus security, and space usage, as well as costs for other important institutional functions such as admissions, record keeping, administration, and yes, parking, are also real. Usually you do not need to link all the detailed costs for services provided by other sectors of the institution to specific academic programs or units. But it is possible to estimate that in the aggregate a certain percent of all income (INC) generated from student enrollments in academic programs is needed to pay for important institutional support services.

At my prior institution, Kent State University, the aggregate of expenditures (EXP) of the academic colleges was 59% of income generated from student enrollments in the courses offered through those colleges in fiscal year 1996. Does this mean that 41% of the income generated was devoted to "needed" services provided to the academic colleges by other sectors of the institution? While this question might generate debate, I assume for purposes of the current discussion that aggregated expenditures within the academic units totaled 60% of the income generated through student enrollments in those units. What does this mean for you? It may mean that the continuing base budget of the college (which I am presuming to be approximately equal to year-end expenditures for the college) should be about 60% of the income (INC) generated from enrollments in academic programs (units) within the college. Thus if the EXP/INC ratio for some programs (units) in the college is greater than six-tenths (6 EXP/10 INC), then EXP/INC ratios for other academic programs need to bring the aggregate EXP/INC ratio for the college to about six-tenths.

PERFORMANCE MEASURES

The ratio of academic program costs to income generated (EXP/INC) might be described as a fiscal "performance measure" for academic programs. This ratio might also be thought of as an indirect performance measure for collections of faculty involved in particular academic programs. As a program performance measure, the EXP/INC ratio is related to a series of questions. Are the faculty who are responsible for an academic program serving enough students in courses? Do the retention rates for specific academic programs need improvement? Are there enough students in upper division courses? Are section sizes sufficient at the various levels of instruction? Are the aggregated teaching loads of faculty appropriate? What are the graduation trends for a particular academic program?

EXPECTED AND ACTUAL STUDENT/FACULTY RATIOS

Student/faculty ratios can also be characterized as performance measures for academic programs, and they are connected to income generation (INC) and expenditures (EXP), even though that association may be somewhat abstract.

Establishing "expected" program or unit specific ratios (benchmarks) of "full-time equated students" (FTES) to "full-time equated faculty" (FTEF) can be an effective way of measuring program performance. For example, student/faculty ratios measure more than the number courses a faculty member teaches: they are also an indicator of whether or not classes are sufficiently enrolled.

To illustrate the use of student/faculty ratios as performance measures, I will adopt an approach that is similar to one that has been used for higher education in Virginia. For our purposes, 15 student credit hours per semester is defined to be 1 FTES. Thus 75 student credit hours equals 5 FTES.

Assume a humanities unit (program or department) has a total of 14 budgeted FTEF. Further assume this unit offers three levels of courses and instruction: general studies (GS), baccalaureate (BAC), and master's (MAS). Assigned (benchmark) student/faculty ratios [FTFS/FTEF] for the unit by instructional levels are:

GS, 22/I,
BAC, 18/, and
MAS, 15/1.

Averaged over two semesters (the academic year), this humanities unit generated full-time equated students by instructional levels as follows:

GS, 271.6 FTES,
BAC, 40.8 FTES, and
MAS, 9.0 FTES.

Thus the two semester average for humanities was 321.4 FTES.

The actual student/faculty ratio for this unit was

$$\text{(total FTES)/(actual FTEF)} = 321.4/14 = 23/1.$$

How does this actual student/faculty ratio compare to the expected student/faculty ratio? The answer to this question requires calculations involving the assigned (benchmark) student/faculty ratios by levels. Since the assigned student faculty ratio at the GS level is 22/1, and 271.6 FTES were generated at the GS level, productivity at this level would predict a need for 271.6/22 = 12.3 FTEF. Similarly, productivity at the BAC level would predict a need for 40.8/18 = 2.3 FTEF; and productivity at the MAS level would predict a need for 9.0/15 = 0.6 FTEF. Thus based on actual full-time equated students generated, the assigned (benchmark) ratios

by levels of instruction would predict a need for

$$12.3 \text{ FTEF} + 2.3 \text{ FTEF} + 0.6 \text{ FTEF}$$
$$= 15.2 \text{ FTEF}.$$

The expected overall student/faculty ratio for this department is then

$$321.4 \text{ FTES}/15.2 \text{ FTEF} = 21.1/1.$$

This expected student/faculty ratio of 21/1 compares to the actual student/faculty ratio of 23/1, and the "generated" number of lull-time equated faculty is 15.2 compared to 14 actual full-time equated faculty. When compared with the assigned (benchmark) ratios, we would conclude that this academic unit (and by extension, its faculty) exceeds productivity expectations.

INSTITUTIONAL CITIZENS

Assigned (benchmark) student/faculty ratios *and* EXP/INC ratios provide you with complementary and often reinforcing views of program (unit) productivity. In fact, these two performance measures may be two of the best in assessing the "fiscal vitality" of a collection of academic programs.

While fiscal measures are important, so are other productivity considerations, some of which are not easily quantified. Specifically, the expertise, institutional memory, and commitment of a faculty member who has dedicated many years of service to an institution are invaluable. Such a faculty member may help recruit and advise students as "unofficial" parts of his or her responsibilities. This type of faculty member may help "friend and fund raise" on behalf of the institution, and be involved in significant committee activities.

While quality and quantity are not mutually exclusive, there are some things that are difficult to measure in terms of costs and benefits. The "institutional citizen," whether that person be faculty or staff, is undervalued on most campuses.

You can learn about appropriate compensation levels for faculty by reviewing data from a set of peer institutions. You can use performance measures such as INC/EXP and student/faculty ratios for quantitative assessments of program and unit productivity. But to learn the "real stuff" about the institution, you need to seek out and listen to the institutional citizens. Costs aside, these faculty and staff are at the core of the institution and are largely responsible for its overall success. When an institution is in need, it is the institutional citizens who deliver. That is a real benefit at twice the price.

The Financial Side of Deaning

Fund Raising and Entrepreneurship

Peter A. Facione, Santa Clara University

152

*Resource
Handbook
for
Academic
Deans*

As a new dean, you can expect sooner or later to hear the president say, "The way to assure that your college will thrive is to help raise money for scholarships, endowed professorships, programming, equipment, facilities and the like."

A certainly ineffective, if not foolish and fatal, response is, "The faculty and I believe that the excellence and worthiness of our programs are self-evident to the discerning observer. Thus we seek greater institutional support, for we will not compromise quality. In fact, this institution owes my college a greater share of the budget."

A response more likely to be heard and appreciated goes, "Yes, I'm eager to help raise money to advance the priorities of the total campus, other colleges, and my own college. I would also like to talk about ideas for revenue generating projects and related financial incentives. The college and participating departments can contribute to the common good of the campus and still access a reasonable percentage of the net revenue to support student learning, faculty excellence, and those departmental and college goals that have been approved through the campus planning process."

REVENUE GENERATING PROJECTS

A college has surprising capacities for revenue generation. It controls, within legal and policy limits, the use of its land and facilities, the work and expertise of its faculty and staff, and its academic authority to provide recognized educational programs, research, and services. It may have access to the same or better equipment, telecommunications, and physical support services as many area businesses. These physical and human resources, along with some vision, planning, and start-up capital, can be the basis for launching revenue generating activities that are appropriate to the educational and public service mission of the institution. It takes a measure of business acumen and a dash of leadership to create a system of incentives and marketing strategies that build the quality and reputation of the institution, provide income and educational opportunities for faculty, staff, and students, and offer meaningful, institutionally appropriate, and needed services to client organizations and individuals. Here are a few basic suggestions:

Serve clients' interests, not providers' preconceptions. The conception here is of a self-contained, not-for-profit activity with the potential to return to the department, college, and institution reasonable shares of net revenue after expenses each year. For these activities to be financially viable, one must know the clients' interests and financial capabilities. Do not begin planning from the perspective of what the faculty want to offer, nor by presuming to identify what you think the clients should want to know. Rather, begin by trying to provide them with what they actually have a genuine interest in learning. Think quality first, then add convenience, pricing, delivery, and marketing. A thorough knowledge of what other providers are doing, how they are pricing their activities, and how well your program compares to theirs in terms of educational and service quality are essential, if you are going to present a financially and educationally viable activity.

At no time should you do anything that diminishes the academic quality or reputation of your institution. The costs of such a misadventure are too great for too many other parts of the institutional enterprise. The budgeting for these business-like activities should be separated entirely from the regular tuition support and personnel budgets of the college and institution, and handled instead through a separate fund. Although it may be acceptable practice at some institutions, it would generally be a mistake to divert tuition dollars or institutional general fund resources to these enterprises. If start-up funding is loaned from these sources, there should be a multi-year repayment plan. Finally, the time to begin evaluating the project is after its third cycle, which allows the people involved the time to improve on initial designs and refine their presentations and processes.

Programs and facilities. Liberal arts colleges and professional schools can present lifelong learning enrichment programs, continuing education programs in response to professional development as well as licensure requirements, programs for gifted and talented children and high-school students, returning adult degree completion programs, post-baccalaureate certificate programs such as in technical or professional writing, or contract degree programs for business or institutional clients. Beyond academic programs, the special facilities of a campus often provide revenue generation opportunities, for example: long-term summer rentals of theatrical, performing arts, and TV production facilities; joint use contracts with local cities or youth organizations for access, maintenance, and upgrade, of athletic facilities, stadia, and intramural fields; and summer or weekend rental of classrooms and lecture halls, classrooms, and residence halls as conference facilities.

Land and joint ventures. If your campus has acreage and needs buildings, interesting arrangements are possible with city, county, or state governments or departments, or with local research companies, foundations, utility companies, churches, hotel chains, school districts, or health care providers for construction and joint use of new facilities. New curricular and research programs, service-based learning opportunities, grants, and public service programs can often be linked successfully to such joint ventures. Although it may take more years to cultivate the idea and nurture the political and personal relationships than it will take to actually build and occupy the building, these larger undertakings can be wonderful long-term assets to the community as well as to the college.

Talent. Looking at the talent of the students, faculty, and professional staff, you might consider forming a consulting service aimed at business and institutional clients. Consulting services might focus on leadership development, corporate ethics, philanthropy, international relations, environmental issues, strategic planning, public relations, multi-cultural workplace issues, telecommunications, economic and demographic forecasting, ergonomics, organizational psychology, or technological development. Student talent in the use of computers and the graphic representation of idea can be harnessed creatively in the production of webpages, CD-ROMs, and the like for businesses as well as smaller or less technologically capable not-for-profits in the local area. The talent of student journalists working in print or electronic media might be directed to support the internal communication and staff training needs of area schools, religious, and philanthropic organizations. Although

some of these examples might not yield significant net new revenue, they can be set up so that expenses are covered and students gain valuable educational experiences. This provides some additional salary to key members of the regular and adjunct faculty and staff and does no harm to student recruitment and retention efforts—both of which can be financially beneficial.

FUND RAISING

Fund raising is part cultivating, part asking, part strategic positioning, part promoting, part marketing, and a lot of friend-raising and careful stewardship. The positioning needed to be successful in fund raising is the development of a singular idea or institutional identity that captures the core vision, mission, and goals of the college or institution. Presidents and deans, as leaders, are responsible for the articulation of positioning statements. Positioning links campus strategic planning to institutional and college marketing. Marketing can be thought of as systematically creating the conditions for persons to make contributions to the quality and advancement of the enterprise. Marketing is not manipulation; rather, it is the honest presentation of opportunities to persons who have both the means and the will to contribute to the realization of those opportunities. In cultivating a prospective donor or foundation, you should be marketing the institution in ways that respect and, indeed, depend upon the donor's integrity, intelligence, and free choice. Marketing might be distinguished from promotional and advertising activities which simply aim at getting people to do something fairly immediate, like enroll in classes or make a contribution in direct response to a solicitation.

Cultivating prospective donors. This is the most common and most important way in which you can participate in the total institutional fund-raising strategy. If you are unwilling to step up to this responsibility, you should probably resign. More often than not, once you have had a bit of success in this arena, reinforcement begins to work its sweet seduction. At first there are those ceremonial necessities we all say we despise, the occasional alumni event, the luncheon with the foundation officer, or accompanying the president on a visit to a potential campus benefactor. From there we move into the more sophisticated and challenging aspects of development, including major campaigns and the cultivation of specific donors or foundations.

The president and development director may use your knowledgeable enthusiasm for a given project and the generally academic orientation to draw the donor toward some specific element in the institution that they believe to be an area of real interest and concern for that donor. You are not expected to ask for financial support at this point. In fact, a successful strategic effort with a given donor may require several contacts with that prospect in order to build up a relationship of mutual trust and set the stage for the president or director of development or another donor to actually ask for a gift.

Typically, your role is to convey the significance and potential of the project. With the proper staff support from your Development Office, your participation in the cultivation event will have been discussed ahead of time in a prospect briefing and will be followed afterward with a contact report. The prospect briefing will include giving you information about the persons with whom you would be meeting and the identification of the specific project or projects you are expected to describe. The follow-up, usually prepared by you or by a development staff member who attended the event, will summarize what was discussed and include observations with regard to the prospect's apparent level of interest in what you talked about or in other things the institution might be doing.

Annual drives. The annual drive, including such things as the alumni telephone campaign, seeks smaller gifts, but is mostly about raising participation rates, identifying potential donors who might be moved in the direction of larger gifts with greater cultivation, and general institutional identity development. In these drives numbers of contacts count. Fund-raising directors know that the amount pledged is in direct proportion to the number of people asked. If you have not made your pledge, then you will be less effective on the phone or in motivating students or faculty to participate. So the place to start is with yourself. The money raised through annual drives, although the pledges are small, is tough money to raise because it is earned income after taxes. Contrast that with capital gains income from the sale of stock or real estate, which typically is the source of those larger gifts.

Stewardship. What you do with the foundation grant or personal gift afterward may be more important than the work that went into raising that gift in the first place. People and foundations want to know that their money was used as had been agreed upon. Endowments for professorships and scholarships can be made real to donors if those who benefit from the gift, the professor or the students, communicate with the donor about their work or their educational experiences. Foundations expect reports of how funds have been managed. The kinds of reports that lead to subsequent gifts are those that honestly communicate that the first gift was used as intended, much appreciated, and productive as measured by the quality of the results and the level of institutional commitment to continuing the project beyond the duration of the gift.

Resource Handbook for Academic Deans

SUMMARY

You should think strategically about how external gifts can advance core college goals, how you can present these opportunities to individuals and to philanthropic foundations, and how you can use those gifts that have been received so that they accomplish the intended results and pave the way to subsequent academic improvements and fundraising opportunities.

7

Academic

Publications

ACAD
AMERICAN CONFERENCE OF ACADEMIC DEANS

Faculty Handbook as a Living Policy Document

James L. Pence, St. Olaf College

learned the value of understanding faculty personnel policies early in my career in academic administration. During my year as an ACE Fellow in 1985-86, Tom Emmet, the acknowledged "guru" of faculty handbooks, introduced me to the idiosyncrasies of handbook language. When Tom spoke about "fugitive policies," "estate committees," and the "holy trinity" of faculty contracts ("sunlighters," "twilighters, and "moonlighters"), I was hooked! When Tom defined "normally" and "make every effort" as "handbook weasel words," I listened. When Tom argued that the process of writing or revising a handbook is a dean's task, I paid attention. Those of us who studied under Tom Emmet can recognize an Emmet-inspired faculty handbook by its characteristic outline and the absence of "weasel words." ["Writing a Faculty Handbook: A Two-Year, Nose-to-the-Grindstone Process," *Chronicle of Higher Education*, 1985, 31 (5), 28.]

In my first administrative post, I was assigned responsibility for managing the process of revising the faculty handbook. Relying on Tom's materials and his advice as a consultant, I participated in a comprehensive revision of the faculty handbook, an activity that resulted in substantive change in institutional policy and direction. Reflecting on that experience several years later, I wrote that the "process of revising faculty personnel policies can itself become the stimulus for change, enhancing opportunities for successful programmatic redirection or administrative reorganization" ["Adapting Faculty Personnel Policies," *Managing Change in Higher Education*, ed., D.W. Steeples. New Directions for Higher Education, 71 (Fall 1990), 59-68]. Having completed two comprehensive handbook revisions at two quite different kinds of institutions and having served as a handbook consultant on several campuses, I still believe what I wrote in 1990. Knowing what and when to revise is a critical success factor in the world of deaning. Understanding the faculty handbook as a living policy document helps deans to serve the interests of the faculty and to uphold the mission and goals of the institution.

Over the years I have developed five basic principles about writing and revising faculty handbooks:

Distinguish between contractual provisions and explanation

Faculty handbooks should contain the essential employment policies for the faculty. As I understand the legal issues, the handbook itself is not inherently contractual, but it takes on the force of contract when it deals with individual performance, confers a direct benefit, or imposes a direct obligation. Failure to indicate which policies are intended to be contractual and which are intended to explain administrative matters is problematic. A good source of information on the contract issues of faculty handbooks is *Faculty Employment Policies* by Kent Weeks. (College Legal Information, Inc. Nashville, 1997). A practicing attorney and professor, Weeks has written extensively on faculty contract matters in *Lex Collegii* and other forums. This text is subtitled "A Forms Manual for College Decision Makers" and includes extremely helpful sample policies as well as discussions of handbook issues. On the matter of distinguishing between contract and explanation, Weeks is clear: do it carefully! Another good source is the National Association of College and University Attorneys. The NACUA selected reading series includes collections of articles of interest to handbooks. *Legal*

Issues in Faculty Employment is still a very good reference tool (edited by P. Eames and T. Hustoles, 1989).

Recently I had the opportunity to consult with a fellow dean on revising the handbook at his institution. Having understood the importance of distinguishing between contract and explanation, he worried about the loss of "inspirational" language contained in the current text. He did not want to produce a legalistic document and risk redefining the employment relationship between faculty and the institution in narrow, protectionist terms. I suggested that he preface the contractual portion of the handbook with an "academic vision." In that vision, he can write about the values of the institution that undergird the contractual policies. He can express the institution's desire to use clear policies to attract and retain good faculty. He can address the issues of integrity, quality, and standards from philosophical perspectives. And he can clearly label this section as "explanatory."

In my experience reviewing dozens of faculty handbooks, especially those at liberal arts colleges, the blurring of contract and explanation is the most important issue needing attention.

Be aware of incorporation by reference issues

The AAUP "Redbook" belongs on the shelf of every dean (*AAUP Policy Documents & Reports*. American Association of University Professors, 1995). It also belongs in the hands of every faculty member assigned to work on a faculty handbook revision. My first assignment to a handbook revision committee is "read your own handbook." My second assignment is "read the Redbook." The critical issue with respect to AAUP policies is the one of incorporation by reference. As I understand the legal point of view, reference to an external document may lead to an argument that the document is "incorporated by reference" into the handbook. For example, colleges often cite the AAUP "1940 Statement of Principles of Academic Freedom and Tenure" in faculty handbooks. To clarify the intent of that citation, for example, I urge you, in writing a revised faculty handbook, to quote verbatim the portions of the statement you intend to incorporate or indicate that the entire statement is incorporated by reference. Failure to be clear about the use of external documents leads to confusion and potential conflicts of interpretation.

Reference to an internal document also raises the incorporation by reference issue. My institution allows departments to develop their own "Statements of Professional Activity" to serve as standards for evaluating scholarly and creative activities. Although the statements are not physically included in the faculty handbook, the policy authorizing departments to develop statements is clearly intended to incorporate them. They should be appended to the faculty handbook and defined as "incorporated by reference." In the next printing of the handbook, they will! Reference to academic policies contained in the college catalogue may also raise incorporation issues. To the extent that your institution intends to bind faculty to adhere to catalogue policies, you need to be sure the faculty handbook has a clear statement of institutional practices in incorporation by reference.

You should review your faculty handbooks and look for all references to other documents. Such references should be clearly labeled as "incorporated" or "not incorporated." Failure to be clear may lead to lengthy and expensive litigation.

Be aware of delegation of authority issues

When I review a faculty handbook, I read with two important questions in mind: who decides? Who decides who decides? The lack of clear decision architecture presents formidable problems to deans, especially those who come to a position from outside the institution. The faculty handbook is the right place to deal with delegation of authority issues, both in terms of governance and personnel policies. First, the handbook should contain a clear statement of the authority of the governing board. Second, it should indicate what kinds of authority the board delegates to the president. At one institution I served, the board delegated to the president the authority to award tenure. At another, the board delegated the authority to grant promotions but not award tenure.

The "delegation of authority" issue appears most often in handbook language dealing with personnel decisions. Legal constraints in public colleges prevent the delegation of certain kinds of personnel authority; custom serves a similar purpose in private colleges. Being clear about the differences between "decisions" and "recommendations" is imperative in handbook revision. Kent Weeks deals with this issue at length in *Faculty Decision Making and the Law* (College Legal Information, Inc. Nashville, 1994). This manual is designed to inform faculty about the legal implications of the decisions they make. From both the institutional and the individual perspective, delegation of authority issues are important ones for you to consider.

Minimize the disparity between stated procedure and customary practices

The differences between policy and procedure tend to blur in faculty handbooks. When disputes over matters of interpretation occur, they tend to focus on this difference. Being clear about the separation of policy from procedure is a good idea, especially in the contractual portions of the faculty handbook. In some handbooks, policy sections are physically separated from procedure sections; in others, handbook authors state "this is our policy" and "these are the procedures we use to implement that policy." The extent to which handbooks differentiate between policy and procedure depends a good deal upon issues of campus culture and campus climate.

My concern is that deans work to minimize the disparities between stated procedure and customary practices that have evolved over time. For many understandable reasons, customs evolve in spite of written procedures. I have on occasion been told "We don't care what the handbook says; we have never done it that way." Disparity between stated procedure and custom arises as a result of "handbook tinkering" or willful neglect of continuous review of procedures in force. I have two suggestions for reducing potential liability resulting from disparity between stated procedure and custom:

(1) periodic training and development sessions for department chairs and others involved in implementing procedures; (2) establishing a standing regulation that handbook provisions be reviewed on a continuous basis. In some cases, turning custom into stated procedure solves the problem. In other cases, moving text from contractual sections to explanatory sections satisfies all parties.

Recognize the value of faculty handbooks as stories of institutional culture

I have long believed that colleges are workplaces, organizations, and cultures. Faculty members bring to handbook discussions an expectation that the terms and conditions of employment are clearly stated in handbooks. Workload requirements, reward and benefit systems, and professional development opportunities need to be set forth in user-friendly ways in the handbook. Writing or revising handbooks to recognize only the workplace contexts is to diminish the richness of collegiate life. Organizational issues such as effective faculty-administration communication, internal governance and decision-making, and responsibility for responding to faculty recommendations are critical to the maintenance of a healthy workplace. Using a handbook revision to deal with these issues may be an effective means for you to increase cooperation between faculty and administrators. Cultural issues, by far the most complex and the most interesting, are always embedded in handbooks. The important considerations of values, traditions, and symbols are written and implied in the pages of a faculty handbook.

One of the dangers of the litigious age in which we live, over and above the costs of preventing litigation or dealing with it, is that handbook revisions can fail to acknowledge the importance of campus culture in shaping institutional vision. After 14 years of active involvement with faculty handbooks, I am more convinced than ever that deans need to cultivate, not diminish, the Janus-like features of handbooks. If the contractual sections of handbooks are written or revised *after* the explanatory and philosophical sections are adopted, the faculty and the institution will be better served. Too often, debate occurs over contract language and the philosophy behind the language is invented after the fact, if it is stated at all. Once the institution knows why it values tenure, it can write or revise its tenure policies.

SUMMARY

Faculty handbooks are "living" policy documents. Writing or revising faculty personnel policies can become a useful tool for learning about the institution, planning for its future, clarifying its present, and contextualizing its past. If you embark on a revision process, you can expect a "nose-to-the-grindstone" work load for one and one-half to two years. If done well, though, the outcome will serve the faculty and the institution far beyond that time. A good handbook is a roadmap and a compass, a legal document and a vision statement, a prescription and a description. A good handbook also "lives" and changes as the institution and the people who inhabit it change.

163

College Catalogue

Kathleen Schatzberg, Cape Cod Community College

The college catalogue, more than any other publication the institution produces, represents the official and public stance that the college takes towards its students and all its other constituents. It is a public relations document that will project the personality of the institution and may serve as a vital recruitment tool. It is a reference tool used by faculty, counselors, advisors, and students to determine the opportunities offered students, the rights by which they must live, and the responsibilities demanded of them. At the same time, it is a statement of what the college intends to provide, and from many perspectives. It is a legal document that binds both those who attend and those who labor in the institution. Indeed, it is often referred to as the contract between the college and students.

Before the advent of the technologies with which we are now blessed, the annual or bi-annual ritual of producing a new catalogue was tedious, almost torturous.

Virtually everyone involved in it knew with certainty that as soon as it was printed someone would find something dreadfully wrong with it. Fortunately, new technologies have eased this task considerably, and with well-organized, automated systems, revising the catalogue can be accomplished in the course of regular routines, so that the new catalogue can be produced with a minimum of time and effort. None of the technologies, however, will ever substitute for that final, painstaking, word-by-word proofreading by an individual with enough knowledge of the institution, and its offerings to catch the devilishly small and fiendishly huge errors that even the grandest technology will not prevent. That person is the dean!

Some elements of the catalogue are overarching and will involve you as a member of the senior administrative team that reviews them as a whole. These include the college mission, its history, governance, facilities and academic calendar, and statements on such matters as antidiscrimination policies, commitment to affirmative action principles, or compliance with governmental mandates. There should also be a statement notifying readers that any aspect noted in the catalogue may change before the next catalogue is printed, a necessary statement even though the college may be legally held to the provisions announced in the catalogue.

Other elements of the catalogue are the responsibility of student affairs administrators. The elements that most concern you, however, comprise the bulk of the catalogue and include academic policies and procedures: the degree programs offered and their respective requirements; the listing of individual course offerings; and the listing of the faculty and their credentials. Many catalogues also provide information on formal articulation agreements the institution holds with other institutions. The key to managing the production of these components of the catalogue is to establish a pathway by which changes route inevitably to the catalogue. It also helps to have a particular individual in the academic unit of the institution responsible for overseeing these processes, although in small institutions, there may be no one but yourself to fill that role.

Academic policies and procedures, for instance, are usually changed as a result of committee action. Notifications of such actions then go to various offices and persons on campus who need to implement and communicate these changes. The routing must include the academic administrator or staff person responsible for compiling catalogue revisions. If unfailingly collected in this manner, the actual

revision process for these sections of the catalogue becomes easy. As with all sections of the catalogue, keeping an electronic copy specifically for entering such changes as they occur will also reduce the amount of time needed to produce the revised document.

Likewise, the actions of the curriculum committee should lead to the files for revision of the sections on degree programs and courses. Notice of a new articulation agreement should be communicated in similar fashion, as should hiring, promotion, and other human resources actions that would alter the details of the faculty listings in the catalogue. In short, the design of these communication systems will either ease or complicate the task of producing the catalogue.

One philosophical question about the production of the college catalogue involves what may be some fundamental contradictions concerning its purpose. If the catalogue is to be a statement of the institution's image and style, it will include many photographs, statements of ideals and activities in the broader arena of public life, and a graphical format that communicates a personality. If the catalogue is a contract, many of these features are not needed but the catalogue must be exhaustively detailed and precise. The catalogue-as-contract will include a great deal of material concerning regulation of the institution by governing and accrediting bodies as well as institutional regulations governing students. If the catalogue is to be a reference tool for students and a recruitment tool for the Admissions Office, then it must be inviting and user-friendly. This function of the catalogue, for instance, would definitely include such components as descriptions of articulation agreements that offer students undergraduate transfer or graduate-level opportunities, as well as detailed descriptions of scholarships and services provided for students.

Many publications experts would say that the catalogue that tries to serve all these purposes may not do any of them very well. Most colleges face tough choices with limited resources, however, and therefore try to create a catalogue that does serve all these purposes. No easy answers spring up to resolve this dilemma, but the discussion of what purposes the catalogue serves must precede and frame its production. It is your role to lead this discussion among the faculty who may find the catalogue wanting if they are not included in this debate.

One final note on how the college catalogue will be transformed as we adopt ever more sophisticated technology. It is not unusual now for a college to have its catalogue, or major portions of it, posted on a Web page, allowing for instant access by students, prospective students, and the public-at-large, and allowing also for nearly instantaneous updating. The printed paper catalogue as we have known it may go the way of the 78 RPM record or the computer keypunch card. The same institutions posting their catalogues on the Web may also allow students to access course outlines and other information via computer kiosks or lab stations positioned throughout the campus and even via modem from home. These emerging technologies may enable us to produce electronic college catalogues that communicate the college's social style, include more information with greater accuracy, and do so with an ease we could never have imagined when we groaned at the glaring error spotted when the first carton of new catalogues arrived from the printer.

8

Real Life

RESOURCE HANDBOOK ACADEMIC DEANS

ACAD

AMERICAN CONFERENCE
OF ACADEMIC DEANS

Responding to Criticism

Len Clark, Earlham College

The first and critically important step in responding well to criticism in the dean's role is to hear criticism in the first place. The importance of this step is matched by its difficulty.

Most of us are accustomed to a healthy give-and-take with colleagues. We've also read our own student evaluations through the years and think we're pretty good at making adjustments and keeping our occasional anger to ourselves. This may lull us into believing that these skills are easily transferable to the dean's position.

Colleagues only very rarely will directly criticize you to your face. Lest one lose respect for one's colleagues in recognizing this fact, it's good to remember how enormously exaggerated are our students' perceptions of the power of their professors—attributions of power far beyond the reality. Similarly, teaching faculty very often attribute, sometimes almost unconsciously, enormous power to the dean. This is frightening, and it leads to a

great muting of criticism from which you could benefit.

Often, the only criticism you will hear is second or third hand. The first temptation is anger at this kind of indirect criticism, which is easy to interpret as a lack of respect for you personally and a lack of self-respect as well. Cultivate the habit of considering such criticism, however indirect, as a gift. Develop the habit of always thanking those who are its sources. It really is a gift, the more valuable by its rarity. Criticism of deans does occur explicitly and face to face. Some criticism occurs early and from those who simply have a spirit of candor. But a second and more common occasion for direct face-to-face criticism is when people have finally overcome fear through an accumulated anger or distrust that is already at a dangerous boiling point.

Perhaps our most destructive temptation in responding to criticism is to argue. We don't think we are sounding defensive or demeaning in doing so, because so many of us have been trained to believe that argument with colleagues is a mark of professional respect. We've often been taught that to argue with the position is to respect it; to ignore it or treat it with dismissive politeness is to demean the proposal and the colleague. The problem with this approach is that your colleagues will not interpret your response in this way. Argument by someone in a position of perceived power is almost always seen as bullying and demeaning, and sometimes as defensive as well. Cultivate habits of responding that acknowledge the value of your having heard the criticism, whether or not you are able to agree with some part of it or not.

Tone of voice in responding to criticism is more important than you might imagine from the experience of your "previous life." It's best to imagine that you have a megaphone permanently attached to your mouth. A raised voice that you mean to be merely reasonable inflection can be reported to you later, to your great surprise, as your having "yelled" at a colleague.

Many deans have developed effective strategies of asking for feedback from others, knowing that they will get too little unless they ask for it. Try different styles of wording that seem to be effective in eliciting candid comments. Use your friends and senior colleagues, but also experiment with strategies for finding out how you are perceived by your youngest colleague.

Some phrases that might get you thinking about locutions which might fit your style are:

"I've been operating according to one framework, and you're helpfully suggesting that I back up and try on another frame work. That's very useful. Thanks."

"I know it takes a lot of fortitude to be critical. But I really rely on your perception and on your judgment. How could I be doing better with X issue or person?"

(In a follow-up note) "Thanks for your counsel yesterday. I heard you, and you've helped stimulate some worthwhile rethinking on my part. Thanks for the help."

The virtue that underlies the best responses to criticism is a genuine openness to change. While most of us possess this openness in some measure, because we've gotten old enough to realize how many times others have provided us with insight, this virtue is often countered by our keen sense of needing to be consistent, to lead with an eye to policy, and by pressures to accomplish the objectives that have been set for our office or that we have set for ourselves. Deanships of great value are occasionally tied to the accomplishment of objectives about which one must be single minded, and after the accomplishment of which one goes on to other things. Longer deanships are marked less by a set of concrete program objectives than by an adaptability to changing circumstances that allow you to focus most on the needs and gifts—and judgments—of your colleagues.

TRANSITIONAL LEADERSHIP: THE TEMPORARY PRESIDENT

Charles D. Masiello, Pace University

Leading any institution of higher learning is a complex, difficult, and consuming task. Under normal circumstances, the presidency is both a challenging and demanding role. For those who assume the position on a temporary basis, the complications are increased. For purposes of this discussion, I will assume that you have been appointed temporary president. But my comments should be equally of interest to you if you are dean during a period when someone else has been appointed temporary or interim president.

While the terms "interim president" and "acting president" are often used interchangeably, for the purposes of my discussion here, the following distinction is made: an acting president is one whose term is unspecified, whose duties may not span the full range of those of a regular president, and who most often is chosen from within the organization and may indeed have a joint appointment—for example, a dean who assumes the role of

president for a short period of time and then is expected to return to the deanship. Acting presidents may also be considered candidates for the regular position of president. An interim president, on the other hand, is an individual who is selected from outside the institution and is appointed for a fixed period of time. Such a person may or may not assume all the duties of a regular president but is usually precluded from being a candidate for the position of president. With these distinctions in mind, let us examine the challenges and opportunities that accompany the temporary university president in the transitional leadership role.

TEMPORARY PRESIDENT OR INTERIM PRESIDENT—WHICH IS BETTER?

This is a question that every institution in transition must answer. The response depends on many factors: the projected length of the transition period, the degree of positive change that the temporary person is expected to achieve, the campus climate, the availability of candidates, and the anticipated profile of the future president, as well as the long-term objectives of the Board. Temporary presidents are often indicated when the transition period is expected to be short, where major changes are not expected, when the campus environment is relatively stable, and where an appropriate internal candidate is available. Interim presidents may be preferable when the Board desires significant change and anticipates a longer transition period. In such instances, a well-chosen external candidate, rather than an internal candidate such as yourself, may be better able to withstand the political fallout that regularly accompanies major changes. Such a candidate will be freer to make difficult decisions and prepare the way for the new president by getting thorny issues out of the way before his/her arrival. Moreover, an external candidate will not have to cope with the difficulties of returning to a previous position at the university after making unpopular decisions.

If you are appointed temporary president for your university or college, you will be the bridge between the departing president and the naming of a successor. You will therefore play a pivotal role in determining the future success of the new president and the institution as a whole. If you carry out that role effectively, your time in office can serve to clarify institutional identity, provide breathing space, resolve a particular crisis, diminish conflict between faculty and administration, quell student unrest, and create a more supportive foundation upon which the new president can build. Conversely, if you fail to take your role

seriously, your time in office can do just the opposite, placing both the new president and your institution at risk.

CONDITIONS OF APPOINTMENT

The Board of Trustees, as the ultimate decision making body of the institution, is responsible for understanding the culture of the institution, the current climate, and the present and future needs of the institution. The Board also must identify goals and objectives and develop a clear concept of what they wish you to accomplish while transitional president. You should insist that these expectations be clearly communicated to you. Without such guidance, you will be left to speculate about the true desires of the Board and you are therefore apt to drift. Initial and continuing dialogue between yourself and the Board, together with key administrators, will be a major determinant in your success.

The length of the transition period is largely dictated by the projects that the Board expects you to accomplish and should be clearly made known to the community at the time of your appointment. Generally speaking, it is not a good idea for you to remain as temporary president for more than 12 months, although exceptions may be warranted in specific situations. An effective presidential search will normally require a minimum of four months, and may take considerably longer. Consequently, the transition period is frequently of 6 to 12 months in duration.

A formal announcement of your temporary presidency should be made. The Board should carefully consider the components of such an announcement. At minimum, it should specify the length of the appointment, whether or not you will be a candidate for the regular presidency, and your role in the process of searching for a new president. In addition, the announcement should specify what the Board expects you to accomplish and should invest you with the full power of the presidency, or at least sufficient power to accomplish the assigned tasks. Your relationship to the Board should also be specified. The transition process through the first few months of the permanent presidency should also be described. Communicating such information clearly and widely to the university community will serve to provide direction for the institution and diminish the tendency to stagnate or, conversely, rush things through during the transition.

THE TRANSITION TEAM

Establishing the bridge from one president to another is a difficult and complex process that demands careful planning. When such planning is flawed, the transition can be hampered and damage done to the institution. As soon as it is clear that the incumbent will be leaving the presidency, the Board should establish a transition team and strategy that will carry the whole institution through the first few months of the new president's term. Initially, the transition team can help the institution deal with the anxiety that will inevitably accompany the departure of the current president, formulate the issues that require resolution during your tenure as the temporary president, and identify desirable characteristics of the new transitional and permanent leaders.

There is a tendency to believe that once the permanent president is named, the bulk of the task is complete. Nothing could be further from the truth. At this point, the real work may be just beginning. Presidents cannot lead alone. They need mentoring. The transition team, together with yourself as the person who served as temporary president, and members of the senior administration and the Board, can and should provide valuable guidance to the new president. A transition team that is truly committed to the new president's success can be supportive in discrete ways that enable the new leader to understand the culture of the institution, avoid hidden pitfalls, and exert effective leadership. The ability to succeed as president is often determined within the first year that the person assumes office. A sign of a fruitful transition is frequently the willingness, if not eagerness, of the new president to accept input from other well-motivated colleagues. A person who consistently decides to "go it alone" usually does not bode well for the institution.

JOINT ADMINISTRATIVE APPOINTMENTS

Often acting presidents are chosen from the ranks of senior administrators and hold joint appointments. In your case, this means being both temporary president and academic dean. This poses a number of challenges, which may become insurmountable if the search for a permanent president becomes protracted. An obvious challenge is how to get two jobs done simultaneously. The presidency is a full-time job, and so your previous administrative duties must be assigned to a

173

Real Life

trusted colleague who will still require your guidance.

At the same time, you must distance yourself from your previous role. The transfer of power may prove to be a difficult thing for you to do, either for reasons of circumstance or personality. However, if this distancing is not apparent, it may be difficult for the community to view you as fully vested in the role of president. If you are not a candidate for the permanent position, this should be made clear. In so doing, you will eliminate uncertainty, diminish, and avoid lobbying groups who wish you appointed. You may be called on to make difficult decisions that could have dire political consequences. Indeed some deans acting as president have, prior to accepting the appointment, gained assurance that their employment will be guaranteed after the transition period—a wise precaution!

Even so, returning to your original position may be difficult. Power can be seductive, and the challenges of your old deanly position may no longer seem intriguing. People may view you differently. Friendships that once were strong may have been weakened or destroyed. Decisions made as president may produce opposition and new conditions that will hamper your effectiveness on return to your original position. Confusion between your role as executive and as administrator may also arise. Then, too, you may be drained, emotionally and physically, from the rigors of the presidency. Thus, the transition back

to your original position must be as carefully planned as the transition to the temporary presidency was.

On the positive side, some individuals thrust into joint positions find the experience a stimulating one and an energizing change of pace. New challenges will broaden your perspective by providing enhanced understanding of how the entire university enterprise operates. Opportunities to use your talents and creativity in new and innovative ways also abound. A deeper sense of your own strengths and weaknesses may also be achieved through this experience. Finally, it may open up career possibilities by providing good training for a permanent presidency elsewhere.

SUMMARY

The transition from one president to another may not always require temporary leadership; however, in many instances such leadership can be helpful in providing a period to assess the past and plan for the future. No institution should expect a temporary leader to be a miracle worker, but the right person can help to heal divisions and set the stage for a productive new presidency. The secret is to select wisely, provide full background information, and to be clear about the results expected. A temporary president, when well-chosen and actively supported, can provide a sound bridge from one leader to the next.

WOMEN WHO ARE DEANS, DEANS WHO ARE WOMEN

Linda H. Mantel, Willamette University

In thinking about my assignment of a section for the handbook on "Deans Who are Women," I have found it difficult to sort out the "dean questions" from the "woman questions," so I have decided to look at the situation from both directions. I recommend as useful background reading the reports prepared for the AAC&U by Bernice R. Sandler, with Donna Shavlik and Judith Touchton, particularly *The Campus Climate Revisited: Chilly for Women Faculty, Administrators, and Graduate Students* (1986). The climate is certainly better now than it was a decade ago. The data on numbers of women administrators are more favorable now than they were then, and the frequency of "micro-inequities" in the way women are heard and treated on campus has diminished. However, women deans still face issues relating to expectations, trust and rapport, visibility, isolation and colloquy. Many of these issues will loom large if the woman is new to the institution, or if the institutional culture is such that few women have held positions of authority. A woman chosen from the fac-

ulty, or in an institution accustomed to the presence of women in power, may find that her gender has little to do with the issues that are most pressing.

WOMEN WHO ARE DEANS

Most women who become deans have been departmental trailblazers and faculty leaders earlier in their academic careers (first tenured woman, first woman chair, faculty senate chair, etc.), and thus have been successful despite the campus climate issues. They have already demonstrated their competence, decisiveness, assertiveness, and ability to communicate with both women and men. They have developed a comfortable collegial style and are accustomed to being in the minority in many groups.

Women who are experienced academic leaders may find that they engender a level of trust and rapport beyond that achieved by many men. Even small details, such as arranging the office to be conducive to conversation, can set a tone that inspires confidence. By taking advantage of these skills, a woman newly appointed as dean can build good working relationships. However, if they are the only, or one of a few, senior women officers of the institution, such women may find themselves excluded from informal activities in which business is conducted and working relationships reaffirmed. Taking up golf may not be a bad idea! In addition, the absence of a female role model at the top may lead to uncertainties in areas relating to dress, behavior, interactions with trustees and their spouses, and even the customs revolving about going out to lunch. Advice from knowledgeable women who are long-time staff members can be most useful in dealing with the local social expectations.

DEANS WHO ARE WOMEN

A newly appointed dean needs to have a clear understanding of the institution's expectations—both those of the faculty and those of the administration. A dean, chosen from the faculty, should have such understanding, but an outsider, whether male or female, will have a steep learning curve. In addition, if the new dean is the first woman in a high administrative position, there may be issues of style (collaborative vs. hierarchical), as well as decision-making authority and delegation of responsibility.

A major issue for any new dean, and perhaps particularly so for women, is that of isolation. With whom does a dean have professional colloquy? Relationships with previous faculty colleagues often are altered when one becomes a dean, and if the dean is new to the institution, even those relationships are not available. Other senior officers will have a different set of concerns, and a single dean in an institution might believe, with some reason, that there are no colleagues with whom specific problems and perspectives can be shared. These concerns can be lessened to some extent. For instance, if there are a number of institutions in the local area, a deans' group that meets occasionally for lunch can be a useful outlet for colloquy and information. On specific issues, of course, the ACAD list serves an important function. However, by its very nature, the position of a dean is a lonely one when compared to being a faculty member.

FURTHER THOUGHTS

I believe that many of the issues facing women deans do not differ greatly from those facing men; the institutional history and culture and the fact of being an insider or an outsider are probably as important as the gender of the dean in setting and solving problems, although the subtle social-professional expectations still need to be understood.

On a lighter note, I believe that useful tools for all deans are Mantel's Three Rules of Administration:
1. You can't do everything;
2. You can't win them all;
3. Not everybody will love you all the time (followed by Jacobson's Corollary: And that's OK).

In my experience, I have found that these three rules are particularly difficult for women to follow: we're accustomed to doing everything; if we've come this far, we're accustomed to winning; and of course everyone should love us, that's part of our job! Remembering and obeying these rules when in a sticky situation may help to resolve the dean's current crisis.

Academic Deaning Despite Difference

James P. Pitts, University of North Carolina at Ashville

Academic deans are increasingly expected to exercise leadership in encouraging faculty and administrative staff throughout the college or university to incorporate diversity into personnel recruitment, curriculum, and all aspects of the campus learning environment. Despite a number of legal attacks on affirmative action in the 1990s, colleges and universities continue to make efforts to integrate race and gender diversity into their educational missions and routine practices of operation. But how is the academic leadership situation affected when the college or university hires or promotes an academic dean who represents one or more of the categories of difference that traditionally have been excluded or marginalized in the history of the institution? How is the leadership role of the academic dean affected when he or she is black or female in an institution that traditionally has been governed by whites or males?

For the past decade I have been the new black dean in academic roles heretofore held by white males. I've served as the Associate Dean of Academic Affairs at Ohio Wesleyan, and I've served as the Chief Academic Officer at Manchester College, Albright College, and now at The University of North Carolina at Asheville. The first three are private and the last is the designated public liberal arts university for the 16-campus University of North Carolina system. Incidentally, in my two most recent appointments I have reported to campus leaders (president or chancellor) who are women.

The socially constructed significance of race and gender hierarchy is manifest in the social climate of a given campus and how that campus climate changes. The selection of a woman or African-American academic dean is a significant development in the life and history of a campus where that position has been associated exclusively with white males. For many members of the campus community the incarnation of progressive change in the person of the academic dean is a realization of democratic values, the fulfillment of the best values of the school and the nation. They feel pride in the "moral development" of the university, demonstrated in its transcendence of prejudice and ignorance. Everyone seems elated that selection of the best person for the job resulted in a choice that coincides with a campus triumph for diversity.

Women and people of color, faculty, staff and students, often feel a particular pride in the selection of the new academic dean. They frequently say that they feel affirmed by the selection and look forward to a more inclusive and fair campus climate.

The campus-wide pride and sense of victory that is usually attendant with the selection of a black or woman academic dean turns up the heat on those members of the community, particularly faculty, who are consistent opponents of so-called multiculturalism or affirmative action. Such persons may be correctly labeled or misunderstood. Now in the eyes of their ideological rivals in the campus community, reactionaries are thought to be on the losing side. Such faculty often feel besieged. They may worry that the arrival of the new academic dean devalues whites and males, and that the "new administration" will become the partisan leader of the victorious campus faction.

The primary roles and scope of responsibilities of the academic dean remain the same despite campus issues and conflicts over achieving diversity—to be the chief advocate for academic excellence and student learning. Black and women academic deans have no less responsibility than

white male deans to provide a sense of direction and priorities for the campus and to assure that the various offices and resources of the administration support the academic and broader learning mission of the campus. The particular challenge that confronts the new dean who is black or a female is that your arrival raises campus expectations, positive and negative. These heightened expectations become an additional factor in the dynamics of your campus.

Campus situations vary and there is no foolproof set of rules for the conduct of the new academic dean that will simplify the circumstances of determining how you should lead despite the significance that various campus constituencies attach to your presence. Nonetheless, here are a few tips that you might consider:

1. Stay focused on the campus-wide leadership role of the academic dean; don't be seduced into trying to perform the roles of people who report to you. To be sure, you should be alert to opportunities to correct long-standing inequities and exclusion, but you must learn to be effective by using the language of leadership and the management scope and rewards appropriately exercised by the academic dean.

2. Do a quick and thorough study of campus governance traditions and formal guidelines. These constitute the topology of contested campus terrain. Learn to use them to promote excellence and to accomplish new horizons of fairness. Ignore them and your leadership and agenda will be stillborn.

3. Listen carefully to all constituencies and sources of information but always weigh the validity and partiality of

advice and information. Both "friends" and "enemies" have good reasons to persuade and manipulate you.

4. Exhibit fairness in all your dealings with campus personnel and in moving the academic program toward higher goals. This means that you should be sure that reactionaries are treated fairly. It also means that you should cultivate a climate of mentoring and fairness that will benefit everyone, including women and racial minorities. A college or university cannot assure a fair and supportive environment for women and African-Americans if it has an underdeveloped or even arbitrary human resources infrastructure. Fairness for women and blacks on your campus, if it is to endure, may require fundamental reforms of basic evaluation and reward systems.

5. Finally, be strategic and selective in making changes; the academic dean, even a woman or African-American, is least effective where he or she tries to make changes in many areas and all at the same time. Don't make too many enemies at once.

Real Life

Servant-Leadership: Deans at Church-Related Colleges

James L. Pence, St. Olaf College

At a recent gathering for alumni/ae and friends of St. Olaf College, I was asked to speak in response to the question "Is There a Place for Lutheran Higher Education?" The very fact that graduates of St. Olaf were interested in this question is an important indication of changing times in church-related colleges. Since its founding in 1874 by Norwegian Lutheran immigrants, St. Olaf College has been continuously identified as a "college of the church." The St. Olaf Choir, established in 1912 by F. Melius Christiansen, is internationally known for *a capella* sacred music. More than half of the student body in 1997 self-identified as Lutheran. The president convenes faculty meeting with devotions, and the student congregation holds daily chapel and regular Sunday worship. Not surprisingly, though, our graduates want to know how our church relationship will affect our future.

The diversity of church-related colleges makes generalizing about this sector of higher education very difficult. Defining "church-related" is itself not an easy task! In the sense that I use the term here, I refer to those colleges who self-identify as being in an active relationship with an organized church body. Typically, these colleges express an institutional commitment to keeping alive the dialogue between learning and faith. My comments do not apply, therefore, to colleges that "cherish their historic ties with churches" or "value the traditions of its founders" but are otherwise thoroughly secular.

Having served since 1990 as the chief academic officer at two Lutheran colleges, I have devoted a good portion of my professional reading to the history, traditions, and values of church-related colleges. I meet regularly with deans of church-related colleges in various professional associations, and I interact frequently with Lutheran clergy and lay people who have long personal histories of ties to Lutheran colleges. I have also read widely in the literature of leadership development, a practice I have worked hard to maintain since my 1985-86 year as an ACE Fellow. Based on reading and experience, I believe that church-related colleges offer a distinctive opportunity for deans who view themselves as servant leaders. In academic communities where both learning and faith are highly valued, servant leadership is undoubtedly the most fitting and most effective leadership model.

The servant-leader model manifests itself in three important contexts in church-related colleges: personal, behavioral, and organizational. I offer a separate thesis about each of these contexts.

My first thesis is that deans at church-related colleges both *minister* and *administer*. A pastor friend of mine called my attention to this passage in a book written for the continuing education of clergy:

> *Leadership:* The creation and articulation of, the focusing attention on, and the developing commitment to a vision of what God is calling the congregation to be and to do—and the concrete form its mission in the community should take—marks the excellent parishes. Such leadership is primarily and indispensably exercised by the pastor(s). It is rooted in the pastor's self-awareness of being called by God to exercise the office of ministry and refined by training in the various disciplines and tasks of pastoral ministry. It is exercised through an ordained minister's constant interaction with people in pursuit of bringing the Gospel to bear on their daily lives. (Daniel V. Biles, *Pursuing Excellence in Ministry* (Alban Institute, 1988), 9)

In church-related colleges, deans constantly interact with faculty and students in pursuit of bringing the lessons of learning and faith to bear on daily life. Deans exercise their training in academic disciplines and academic management to provide leadership for the curriculum, the concrete manifestation of the college's mission. They also carry responsibility for inspiring academic vision among faculty and focusing faculty attention on issues of academic integrity. In church-related colleges, integrity often is interpreted as "what God is calling the college to be and do."

My views on academic leadership have been strongly influenced, admittedly, by my theological preferences. Luther's words in "The Freedom of a Christian" inform my understanding of the practice of deaning:

> A Christian is a perfectly free lord of all, subject to none.

> A Christian is a perfectly dutiful servant of all, subject to all.

Not all church-related colleges emphasize the value of academic freedom as much as Lutherans do; not all deans of church-related colleges see themselves as dutiful servants, either. In colleges with church ties, however, the metaphor of dean as minister is apt. In many of these colleges, presidents have historically been ordained pastors of sponsoring denominations and senior faculty members were hired, at least in part, on the basis of their commitment to the faith traditions of the institution. Being personally comfortable with the metaphor and the role is a healthy precondition for success as a dean in a church-related college.

My second thesis is that deans at church-related colleges exercise *moral authority* more than *legal* or *political authority*. A trustee of Wartburg College told me that my job description as dean there was neatly summarized in one phrase: Do what's right and do it right. Sidney Rand, the former president of St. Olaf, once wrote "the administration of the Christian liberal arts college needs to be above all in the hands of educators" ("The Administration of the Christian Liberal Arts College," in *Christian Faith and the Liberal Arts* (Augsburg, 1960) 83). Faculty members at church-related colleges have justifiably high expectations of moral leadership from the chief academic officer, especially in personnel decisions. While deans everywhere are expected to understand legal constraints and know how to negotiate "the art of the possible," deans in this sector of higher education are expected to lead by "walking the talk."

182

*Resource
Handbook
for
Academic
Deans*

In all sectors of higher education, moral issues should be at the center. Pursuit of the truth does, after all, require moral action. A recent article in *Trusteeship* makes this point well: "Colleges and universities must respect the moral imperative, demanding truth in disciplinary studies and research, as well as in their institutional self-representations" (Thomas E. Corts, "Let's Stop Trivializing the Truth," January/February 1997, 6). Another article in the same issue advises that "college officials must be willing to use moral outrage as an instrument of quality assurance" (E. Grady Bogue, "Moral Outage & Other Servants of Quality," 11). At church-related colleges, however, moral issues are fundamentally mission issues, and academic leaders are more than moral watchdogs. Deans provide the moral compass for academic decision-making. In some educational settings, private behavior and public behavior of administrators can be and often are separated. That is not the case for deans in church-related colleges, nor should it be.

My third thesis is that deans at church-related colleges make *decisions for the common good.* They approach their jobs with the assumption that the whole is greater than the sum of its parts. In *Common Fire*, Sharon Parks and her colleagues write about ways to "kindle a common fire and forge a new synthesis of practical wisdom" in an increasingly complex world (S. Parks, L. Daloz, I. Keen, C. Keen, *Common Fire: Lives of Commitment in a Complex World* (Beacon Press, 1996). 13). The book describes a study of people who lead committed lives dedicated to the common good:

> Such people have learned to trust appropriately and act with courage, to live within and beyond tribe in affinity with those who are other, to practice critical habits of mind and responsible imagination, to manage their own mixed emotions and motives, and to live with a recognition of the interdependence of all life—manifest in a paradoxical sense of time and space. They help us imagine ways of building a more promising future. (19)

Deans who serve at church-related colleges very likely have a strong sense of vocation, being "called" or "sent" by an outside force to complete a task or mission. Church-related colleges are usually small and often located in rural locations, contributing to the powerful sense of community. The combination of vocation and community encourages leaders to value good stewardship, which manifests itself in decision-making focused on the well being of the college as a whole.

Disciplinary loyalty exists in creative tension with institutional loyalty in most colleges. Deans are often called upon to negotiate conflicts between individual or departmental interests and college-wide needs. Church-related colleges are concerned about students and faculty in matters of mind, body, and spirit. Not surprisingly, then, deans in these kinds of schools give preference to the view that "everyone counts" and make decisions in accordance with those preferences. The reality of service as a dean in a church-related college is that the concern for the well-being of the organization as a whole is a necessary and desirable characteristic.

Being a dean at a church-related college is not for everyone who aspires to be a dean. To those who seek positions in these kinds of collages, I offer three pieces of advice:

First, read broadly about church-related higher education. Two recent books I recommend are George Marsden's *The Soul of the American University* (Oxford University Press, 1994) and *Models for Christian Higher Education*, edited by Richard Hughes and William Adrian (William B. Eerdmans Publishing, 1997). Marsden discusses the ways in which religious perspectives have shaped the intellectual contexts of American colleges and universities. He traces the influence of religion in the founding of public and private institutions and provides a context for interpret-

ing the movement "from protestant establishment to established nonbelief." Marsden's book deals with the kinds of issues that deans of church-related colleges face on a regular basis, especially in those colleges where the religious identity is being re-examined or re-invented.

The Hughes-Adrian edition contains essays from scholars at 14 different institutions in seven denominational traditions. The author of each essay was asked to write from an historical perspective and describe how his or her institution "has sought to address the relation between faith and learning from the founding of the institution to the present" (2). In addition to the 14 institutional essays, the volume contains essays on the contribution of the several denominational traditions to American higher education.

Second, study the ethos of the institution as it focuses on institutional sagas, founding documents, and the implicit understanding of the ties with the sponsoring church body. Geography and ethnic identity are often significant factors in the founding of church colleges. Deans who come "from the outside" to serve in these kinds of colleges need to learn the territory early and "read the maps" often. I did not graduate from Wartburg or St. Olaf; I am not German and have only a touch of Norwegian ancestry; and I did not grow up Lutheran. Spending some time reading the archival documents of each institution, meeting with emeriti/ae in intimate off-campus settings, and getting acquainted early on with local pastors and alumni/ae helped me make "real-time" connections to the institutions. The fact that I have been an active member of Lutheran congregations in the communities where I have lived has had an undeniably positive effect on my service as dean. Being able to support the religious ties of the college with conviction and sincerity has been an advantage for me; more importantly, it has increased my job satisfaction and given me an opportunity to deepen my sense of vocation.

Third, understand the theological foundations of the church with which the college is affiliated. Professors who teach at church-related colleges and students who attend them may not be theologically literate. The same should not be said for deans. In the case of Wartburg and St. Olaf, Lutheran theological values are expressed in organizational culture. The Lutheran emphasis on vocation and Luther's concepts of the two kingdoms and the priesthood of all believers undergird institutional practices and inform core values. Lutheran perspectives on Christian humility influence the way we do marketing (or don't do it!). Even if I were not a Lutheran, I would study the Lutheran expression of Christianity while serving as dean at a college with Lutheran ties. I would do this *especially* if I were not a Lutheran.

At the St. Olaf alumni/ae gathering I referred to in my opening paragraph, I identified six challenges for Lutheran higher education at the dawn of the 21st century:

1. Maintaining a clear identity in the competitive higher education marketplace, especially in a post-denominational era and in a society where "church-related" is not, as it once was, associated with quality in education. "Because we are church-related, we are suspect," a respected senior professor said to me recently.

2. Recruiting a diverse student body to an academic community that values religious expression.
3. Recruiting talented faculty members who support the mission and goals of the college with conviction.
4. Controlling costs to insure access for students from economically diverse backgrounds.
5. Managing change without destroying positive elements of institutional ethos.
6. Communicating the value of smallness and the integrity of church-related education in a secular society that appreciates bigness and thinks of the separation of church and state as "American."

I also identified six prescriptions for a healthy and productive future:

1. Faithfulness to mission is more important than reputation.
2. Clarity of purpose, goals, and priorities is good stewardship.
3. Embracing diversity is morally responsible.
4. Celebrating academic freedom is our distinctive heritage.
5. Collaboration with other church-related agencies makes sense.
6. Keeping alive the dynamic tension between faith and learning is our distinctive niche.

Although I spoke about St. Olaf as a college of the Lutheran church, my lists of challenges could apply equally as well to many church-related colleges. My list of prescriptions, on the other hand, is less broadly applicable.

It may be the case that the theses I propose and the advice I have offered are broadly applicable to deans newly appointed to or developing interest in positions in church-related colleges. On the other hand, they may apply only narrowly. Generalizing about church colleges is as dangerous as generalizing about deaning. I am convinced, however, that being a dean in a church-related college affords a rich opportunity to practice servant leadership in meaningful and satisfying ways. It has allowed me to be openly and unambiguously passionate about the two institutions for which I care most deeply: the college and the church. Those of you who share that passion will find church colleges very good places to be, and church colleges will appreciate finding you.

Real Life

Helping Your Successor

George Allan, Dickinson College

This too shall pass away. Someday it'll happen: you'll accept a deanly position elsewhere, return to the faculty, become a president, retire, join the Army, whatever. When that happens, what obligation if any do you have to your successor? That person might be the heir apparent whom you had hand-picked, or the person who drove you from office, or someone not even selected by the time of your departure. I recommend a Kantian answer: you should ignore such happenstance and do precisely those things that you would want anyone else in a similar situation to do.

This admonition can be operationalized as follows: you should do for your successor precisely as you wish your predecessor had done for you. First, repeat those things you appreciated your actual predecessor having done in preparation for your appearance on the scene. Second, do not repeat whatever your predecessor did that proved useless, counterproductive, or an outright hindrance to your efforts.

Third, add those things of which your predecessor unfortunately gave you no forewarning but could have.

THINGS TO DO

Here are at least a few things you should do:

1. Create a checklist of the immediate next tasks to be done: previously scheduled new business, as well as the unfinished business you are simply not going to be able to move to the outbox before you leave. Some of these matters will be more important than others, but they will all need the new dean's early attention. Since your successor will be dealing with these issues while waiting for the new paint job on the office to dry and before he/she is quite clear where the bathrooms are, it would help to provide where possible an outline of the course of action you would have taken or the options as you see them. The new dean may wish

to ignore your suggestions completely, but you might save that person a lot of wasted time and even embarrassment by pointing the way through what may still seem to his/her new eyes a confusing maze of enigmas enwrapping booby traps.

2. Provide a calendar and tickler file for the yearly dean's office cycle of responsibilities. What's important here is not the details but the facts: by when does what need to be done? Better yet, simply let the new dean inherit your office manager or secretary: the one who actually makes the tickler file work. The new dean may want to change some of the practices underlying the yearly office calendar, but you should assume he/she will be wise enough to follow advice implied throughout this handbook and for the first year follow your old calendar of routines.

3. Indicate which committee files need to be carefully perused in advance of the new dean showing up to his/her first meeting of each committee. This information should include the decisions or recommendations that came from the committee during the past year, the minutes of those meetings, and the crucial documents used in arriving at its actions.

4. Provide well-ordered files on departments, programs, and institutes, etc., under the dean's purview. Each should include a history of what's happened to the entity in question, including information on the dean's interactions with it over recent years, a portrait of its current status, and an indication of its expectations and aspirations, especially anything that might be taken as a promise that you've made or that

was made by the faculty or administration but which has not yet been kept. This category of "promises" is especially important because departments and their ilk are sometimes tempted to imagine promises that a former dean (that's about to be you) made to them, or to discover that promises really made to them by that former dean have been unaccountably forgotten by others, especially by collegial competitors.

5. Similarly, provide well-ordered files on individual faculty members. Depending on the number of faculty for whom you are dean, this set of files should encompass either all of the faculty or at least the important ones (the best scholars, the best teachers, the best "campus citizens," the chairs, the key committee members, representative younger faculty, representatives of key special interest groups). Each file should contain a history of the person's evaluations, a salary history, and some indication of his/her aspirations (perhaps in the form of self-evaluation statements), and an indication of promises made but not yet kept.

6. Be sure that you have a detailed paper trail available for the new dean on all legally sensitive matters. In particular, include a paper trail on all personnel decisions for which the dean has responsibility even if only pro forma. My view is that the more detail the better, but this is contrary to some lawyers who recommend having as minimalistic a paper trail as possible. The point here is that the procedural and substantive decisions made while you were responsible for things are about

to be your successor's responsibility. So be sure that person knows as fully as possible that for which he/she has just become responsible, and may you never be called back to testify in court.

7. Collect together in one place the relevant institutional and deanly "vision things" such as
   - ❖ Long range planning documents
   - ❖ Mission statements
   - ❖ Self-studies for accrediting agencies and the formal evaluation reports
   - ❖ White papers
   - ❖ Presentations made by the president and by yourself, that express judgments about the past of the institution (all of it or some segment of it) and sketch aspirations regarding its future.

Your successor may hope to remain loyal to that tradition and that vision (those intertwining traditions, those clashing visions) or to break with it sharply. Or, in Hegelian fashion, your successor may wish to save the best of the old by cutting away its worst, remolding what remains in the light of a new sense of importance and opportunity. In any case, your successor will need to become familiar with the old ways in which your institution has understood itself. Put this stuff front and center on the new dean's desk: label it "Required Orientation Reading."

These suggestions simply come down to an admonition to keep good records. If you retain pertinent information (not too much, not too little: just the right amount and kind of stuff) about the academic program and the faculty, the existence of that information in accessible and intelligible

form will be the best way to have prepared for your successor. So from your first day as dean you should be laying the groundwork for a smooth transition to an unknown successor.

THINGS NOT TO DO

Now let me be negative and indicate some things not to do for your successor. These are things you might well be tempted to do. Well, don't!

1. Don't provide the new dean with your personal views on the virtues and vices of administrative and faculty colleagues. No gossip about good guys/bad guys, please. Your successor will find out soon enough who they are. Remember that your devils may be your successor's saints, and those who are inherently unredeemable will soon enough reveal themselves. Meantime, your departure is like the first day of spring. It's a new world now, and there may be those who will use the occasion to turn over a new leaf, to put a long-festered grievance against the dean's office behind them and treat the new dean kindly. Honeymoons are important: don't poison the well with your prejudiced assessments (whether they be right on the mark or wide of it, they are still, for someone not yet arrived on campus, prejudgments).

2. Don't tie your successor's hands by making irreversible decisions on controversial matters, decisions with which it would be reasonable to imagine your predecessor not agreeing. In other words, don't try to lock in your accomplishments in fear that otherwise they will not survive your

departure. The future is no longer yours: don't try to preempt it. (This is not in contradiction with the Point 3 below!).

3. Don't put off difficult decisions, shoving them off on your successor, because you find the task unpleasant. The more you can take on the burden of making the "hard choices" needed to bring old projects to a close or simply to continue effectively the flow of established practices, the more you give your successor the gift of breathing room. Your successor's day for hard choices will come soon enough; as far as possible, let it be as a result of prior decisions made by that person, not by you.

◆ ## A CLOSING THOUGHT

Let me close with a brief panegyric on institutions. The citadel of higher learning where I spent my career has lines in its alma mater that could be modified as follows: "oh deans may come, and deans may go, but this noble college shall long endure." The office of the dean is more important than you are. Even though without you that office would be an empty shell, without it you are just another Joe or Jane. Act always with an eye on the office and the purposes for which it exists. Be sure that what you received as a trust you will be able to pass on as a trust, preferably one you have helped alter in the meantime for the better. Use the office always and only for the good of your institution, and then hope that you will find that good to have served your own good as well. Your best gift to your successor is to have lived by this sort of an ideal of the office you have chosen to serve.

189

Real Life

List of Resources

WHAT A DEAN IS

National Organizations:

American Conference of Academic
Deans (ACAD)
Contact Eliza Jane Reilly
Executive Director
1818 R Street
Washington, DC 20009
(202) 387-3760
(202)265-9532 FAX
Dean's List: reilly@aacu.nw.dc.us

About ACAD:

"The American Conference of
Academic Deans' objective is to
encourage, initiate, and support
programs and activities that enhance the academic stature and the
public understanding of liberal education. ACAD provides opportunities
for academic deans to meet, exchange views, and discuss common
problems of higher education related
to the arts and sciences in colleges
and universities. Now in its 55th
year, ACAD currently serves 600
deans from public and private colleges and universities throughout
the United States. All academic
deans and chief academic officers,
both graduate and undergraduate,
are eligible for membership."

Council of Colleges of Arts and
Sciences (CCAS)
College of Arts and Sciences
Arizona State University
P.O. Box 873901
Tempe, AZ 85287-3901
(602) 727-6064

About CCAS:

"The Council of Colleges of Arts and
Sciences is a national association
of baccalaureate degree-granting
colleges of arts and sciences whose
purpose is to sustain the arts and
sciences as the leading influence in
American higher education. The
Council serves as a forum for the
exchange of ideas and information
among deans of arts and sciences
representing the member colleges
and as a representative of the liberal
arts and sciences at a national
policy-making level. The Council
further seeks to support programs
and activities to improve the intellectual stature and public understanding of the disciplines of the
arts and sciences."

Council of Independent Colleges (CIC)
One Dupont Circle, N.W., Suite 320
Washington, DC 20036
(202)466-7230
(202)466-7238 FAX
Website: www.cic.edu

About CIC:

"The Council of Independent Colleges is an international association of more than 400 independent, liberal arts colleges and universities. CIC works with college presidents, academic deans, other administrators, and faculty to help its member institutions enhance educational programs, improve their administrative and financial performance, and increase their institutional visibility. The Council is known as both a source of practical advice for college leaders and a resource of ideas for educational reform."

Society of Academic Officers (SAO)
SAO is a division of the Center for Policy in Higher Education (CPHE)
4301 Connecticut Avenue, Suite 450
Washington, DC 20008
phone: (202) 363-3149
fax:(202) 363-6598
e-mail: info@cph.org or sao@cphe.org
web:http://www.cphe.org

About SAO:

"To provide professional development, networking opportunities, and a forum for the exchange of ideas for academic administrators from all types of institutions and levels of the profession."

Strategies:

From Douglas Steeples, Mercer University:

"Materials that Deans should read with care.

❖ These include the college bulletin or catalogue, the viewbook, and other admissions materials:
 ◆ complete a "course count: as a means of getting a curricular overview;
 ◆ complete a staffing diagram to get a sense of how your human resources are allocated;
 ◆ frame an understanding of whom the institution seeks to recruit as students and how they do this.
❖ The minutes for at least the most recently completed academic year, of the faculty business meeting or that of the faculty senate.
❖ The records/recommendations of any committees on faculty recruitment, promotion, and tenure, together with those of your predecessor.
❖ The records for the past year of any other committees that work closely with you.
❖ The faculty handbook, especially those portions pertaining to the practices in place for recruiting, promoting, and tenuring faculty colleagues, and those pertaining to faculty responsibilities, and to processes for changing the curriculum.
❖ The most recently completed accreditation self-study report, and written responses and recommendations from your regional accrediting body.
❖ The budgets for your college or school at least for the current and the most recent year, and, if possible, 3 to 5 years, in order to ascertain funds.

❖ Audited financial statements for your college or school.

❖ Any written materials concerning budge planning procedures and processes, and policies governing fiscal management.

❖ Any college, school, or (especially) presidential planning documents."

BECOMING A DEAN

Publications:

Martin, Joseph. *To Rise Above Principle: The Memoirs of an Unreconstructed Dean*. Urbana/Champaign, Illinois: University of Illinois Press, 1988.

Tucker, Allan and Robert Bryan. *The Academic Dean: Dove, Dragon, and Diplomat*. Washington, DC: ACE, 1988.

See list of Resources on Administration and Management, Higher Education, Serial Publications, the Classics, and Good Novels and Entertainments provided by Sam Hines on pages 47-52.

Publishers:

Jossey-Bass, ACE/Macmillian/Oryx, Johns Hopkins, and Anker Publishers

CURRICULUM

Publications:

Chandler, John et al. *Liberal Learning and the Arts and Sciences Major*, 2 volumes. Washington, DC: Association of American Colleges, 1990.

Curtis, Mark H. et al. *Integrity in the College Curriculum*. Washington, DC: Association of American Colleges, 1985.

Gaff, Jerry G., James Ratcliff, and associates. *Handbook of the Undergraduate Curriculum*. San Francisco: Jossey-Bass, 1997.

Kells, H.R. *Program Review and Educational Quality in the Major*. Washington, DC: Association of American Colleges, 1992.

Kells, H.R. *Self-Study Processes: A Guide to Self-Evaluation in Higher Education*. 4th ed. Phoenix, Arizona: American Council on Education/Oryx Press, 1995.

Orrill, Robert. ed. *Education and Democracy: Re-Imagining Liberal Learning in America*. New York: College Entrance Examination Board, 1997.

Schneider, Carol Geary and Robert Shoenberg. "Contemporary Understanding of Liberal Education: the Academy in Transition." Washington, DC: Association of American Colleges and Universities Publications, 1998.

Strategies:

From Peter Alexander, St. Peter's College:

"On Curriculum Review: Our earlier cycles (all departments in a 5-year rotation) were comprehensive; i.e., each department had to evaluate everything. Current and future cycles will be focused, each on a different theme. For example, the current cycle is focused on Outcomes Assessment. The intent is to have fewer issues to deal with in the hope of getting better and more in-depth analysis."

LEGAL MATTERS

Publications:

Bowen, William B. And Derek Bok. *The Shape of the River: Long-Term Consequences of Considering Race in College and University Admissions.* Princeton: Princeton University Press, 1998.

"Sexual Harassment: Suggested Policy and Procedures for Handling Complaints." Policy Documents and Reports. Washington, DC: American Association of University Professors, 1991.

Eames, P. and T. Hustoles. *Legal Issues in Faculty Employment.* Washington, DC: The National Association of College and University Attorneys, 1989.

Fitzgerald, L. *Sexual Harassment in Higher Education: Concepts and Issues.* Washington, DC: National Education Association, 1992.

Paludi, M. *Ivory Power: Sexual Harassment on Campus.* Albany, N.Y.: State University of New York Press, 1991.

Weeks, Kent. *Faculty Decision Making and the Law.* Nashville, Tennessee: College Legal Information, Inc., 1994.

Weeks, Kent. *Faculty Employment Policies.* Nashville, Tennessee: College Legal Information, Inc., 1997

Publishers:

College Legal Information, Inc. publishes *Lex Collegii,* a quarterly legal newsletter for independent higher education institutions.

ACADEMIC PUBLICATIONS

Publications:

Chronicle of Higher Education. "Writing a Faculty Handbook: A Two-Year, Nose-to-the-Grindstone Process." 1985. 31 (5).

Pence, James L. "Adapting Faculty Personnel Policies." D. W. Steeples, ed. *Managing Change in Higher Education.* New Directions for Higher Education, 71 (Fall 1990).

Publishers:

American Association of University Professors. AAUP Policy Documents and Reports.

Strategies:

From James L. Pence, St. Olaf College:

"In my experience reviewing dozens of faculty handbooks, especially those at liberal arts colleges, the blurring of contract and explanation is the most important issue needing attention."

"You should review your faculty handbooks and look for all the references to other documents. Such references should be clearly labeled as "incorporated" or "not incorporated." Failure to be clear may lead to lengthy and expensive litigation."

"Disparity between stated procedure and custom arises as a result of "handbook tinkering" or willful neglect of continuous review of procedures in force. I have two suggestions for reducing the potential liability resulting from disparity between stated procedure and custom: (1) periodic training and development sessions for department chairs and others involved in implementing procedures; (2) establishing a standing regulation that handbook provisions be reviewed on a continuous basis. In some cases, turning custom into stated procedures solves the problem. In other cases, moving text from contractual sections to explanatory sections satisfies all parties."

REAL LIFE

Publications:

Biles, Daniel V. *Pursuing Excellence in Ministry.* Berkeley, CA: The Alban Institute, 1988.

Bogue, E. Grady. "Moral Outrage & Other Servants of Quality." Trusteeship. January/February, 1997.

Corts, Thomas E. "Let's Stop Trivializing the Truth." Trusteeship. January/February, 1997.

Hughes, Richard and William Adrian. *Models for Christian Higher Education.* Grand Rapids, Michigan: William B. Eerdmans Publishing, 1997.

Marsden, George. *The Soul of the American University.* Oxford, England: Oxford University Press, 1994.

Parks, Sharon and L. Daloz, I. Keen, and C. Keen. *Common Fire: Lives of Commitment in a Complex World.* Boston: Beacon Press, 1996.

Rand, Sidney. "The Administration of the Christian Liberal Arts College." Christian Faith and the Liberal Arts. Minneapolis: Augsberg, 1960.

Sandler, Bernice and Donna Shavlik and Judith Touchton. *The Campus Climate Revisited: Chilly for Women Faculty, Administrators, and Graduate Students.* Washington, DC: American Association of Colleges and Universities, 1986.

Strategies:

From Len Clark, Earlham College:

"Cultivate the habit of considering... criticism, however indirect, as a gift. Develop the habit of always thanking those who are its source. It is really a gift, the more valuable by its rarity."

From Linda H. Mantel, Willamette University:

"Mantel's Three Rules of Administration:

1. You can't do everything;
2. You can't win them all;
3. Not everybody will love you all the time (followed by Jacobson's Corollary: And that's ok)."

From George Allan, Dickinson College:

"...you should do for your successor precisely as you wish your predecessor had done for you. First, repeat those things you appreciated your actual predecessor having done in preparation for your appearance on the scene. Second, do not repeat whatever your predecessor did that proved useless, counterproductive, or an outright hindrance to your efforts. Third, add those things of which your predecessor unfortunately gave you no forewarning but could have."

"These suggestions come down to an admonition to keep good records. If you retain pertinent information (not too much, not too little: just the right amount and kind of stuff) about academic program and the faculty, the existence of that information in accessible and intelligible form will be the best way to have prepared for your successor. So from your first day as dean you should be laying the groundwork for a smooth transition to an unknown successor."

Contributors

Chairs, ACAD Board

1992 Tamar March, New England College
1993 Len Clark, Earlham College
1994 Margaret Curtis, Albion College
1995 Hannah Goldberg, Wheaton College
1996 Lloyd Chapin, Eckerd College
1997 Bari Watkins, Morningside College
1998 David Leary, University of Richmond

H. Dale Abadie is currently the Associate Director of The Croft Institute for International Studies, University of Mississippi. He formerly was Dean of the College of Liberal Arts at the University of Mississippi.

Peter Alexander is Academic Dean at Saint Peter's College.

George Allan is currently Professor of Philosophy Emeritus at Dickinson College. He formerly was Dean of the College at Dickinson.

Lloyd W. Chapin is Vice President and Dean of the Faculty at Eckerd College.

Len Clark is Provost and Academic Dean at Earlham College.

Virginia Coombs is Vice President of Academic Affairs at Oklahoma City University.

Martha A. Crunkleton is Professor of Philosophy and Religion at Bates College. She formerly was Vice President for Academic Affairs and Dean of the Faculty at Bates.

Peter A. Facione is Dean of the College of Arts and Sciences at Santa Clara University.

Philip Glotzbach is Vice President of Academic Affairs at the University of Redlands.

Myron S. Henry is Provost and Professor of Mathematical Sciences at the University of Southern Mississippi. He was formerly Provost and Professor of Mathematics at Kent State University.

Samuel M. Hines, Jr. is Dean of Humanities and Social Sciences and

Professor of Political Science at the College of Charleston.

David Hoekema is Interim Vice President for Student Life and Professor of Philosophy at Calvin College. He was formerly Academic Dean at Calvin College.

David E. Leary is Dean of the School of Arts and Sciences at the University of Richmond.

Carol E. Lucey is Vice President for Academic Affairs at SUNY College of Technology at Alfred.

Linda H. Mantel is Interim Vice-President for Academic Administration at Willamette University. She was formerly Dean of the Faculty at Reed College.

Gary L. Maris is Professor of Political Science at Stetson University. He was formerly the Dean of the School of Arts and Sciences at Stetson.

Charles D. Masiello is Dean of Dyson College of Arts and Sciences at Pace University.

James L. Pence is Vice President and Dean of the College at St. Olaf College.

James P. Pitts is Vice Chancellor for Academic Affairs at the University of North Carolina at Asheville.

Lisa A. Rossbacher is President of Southern Polytechnic State University. She was formerly Dean of the College at Dickinson College.

Elizabeth Scarborough is Dean of Liberal Arts and Sciences at Indiana University South Bend.

Kathleen Schatzberg is President of Cape Cod Community College. She was formerly Vice President for Academic Affairs at Rochester Community and Technical College.

Douglas Steeples is Dean and Professor of History of the College of Liberal Arts at Mercer University.

Walter C. Swap is Dean of the Colleges at Tufts University.

Bari Watkins is Vice President and Dean of the College at Morningside College.